# PROCEDURES, PRACTICE AND GUIDANCE FOR SENCOs

## HAZEL SMITH

A NASEN Publication

Published in 1996

© Hazel Smith

ISBN 0 906730 76 7

Published by NASEN Enterprises Ltd.
NASEN Enterprises is a company limited by guarantee, registered in England and Wales. Company No. 2637438.

Further copies of this book and details of NASEN's many other publications may be obtained from the Publications Department at its registered office: NASEN House, 4/5, Amber Business Village, Amber Close, Amington, Tamworth, Staffs. B77 4RP.
Tel: 01827 311500; Fax: 01827 313005

Copy editing by Nicola von Schreiber.
Cover design by Graphic Images.
Typeset in Times by J. C. Typesetting and printed in the United Kingdom by J. H. Brookes, Stoke-on-Trent.

# PROCEDURES, PRACTICE AND GUIDANCE FOR SENCOs

## Contents

3

4

# Acknowledgements

The author wishes to express her thanks to the NASEN Publications Sub-Committee for their useful advice, and in particular to Mike Hinson for his support and encouragement.

The author wishes to make it clear that the views expressed in this publication are her own views and not necessarily those of the Cumbria LEA.

# Introduction

This book is for those special educational needs co-ordinators (SENCOs) who are trying to juggle the demands of their role and management responsibilities within the time available. It aims to offer practical advice on how to carry out the day-to-day work of the SENCO and provides proformas on which to build documentation.

The *Code of Practice* has raised the profile of special educational needs (SEN) once again. It has placed an increased accountability on schools and governing bodies to provide support for pupils with SEN and to produce evidence of how resources are used. Many of the requirements of the *Code* are no more than the good practice which has always existed, but increased demands have undoubtedly been placed on SENCOs, particularly in relation to documentation and records, Individual Education Plans (IEPs) and review procedures. In some schools, particularly primary, the role of SENCO is a newly identified one and the teacher designated to take on this responsibility may not feel confident to respond to the demands of the post.

In order for you to be able to respond to the demands of the SENCO role and to be able to provide the best support for pupils with SEN, the following are essential:

- the awareness of the governing body of their responsibility in relation to special needs;
- the support of the headteacher and senior management, in terms of the status of the post, time to carry out the duties, and appropriate resources;
- the acceptance of the staff that they all have a shared responsibility to provide for pupils with SEN.

You may feel that you have some way to go to achieve these, but in working with staff and governors to develop a whole school response to special educational needs you should, hopefully, be moving towards these ideals.

# A Summary of the *Code of Practice*

The *Code of Practice on the Identification and Assessment of Special Educational Needs* (DfE, 1994) provides practical guidance to local education authorities (LEAs) and governing bodies of all maintained schools on their responsibilities for pupils with SEN as set out in the *Education Act 1993*. The *Code* came into effect on 1 September 1994, and since that date LEAs, schools and other agencies who help them to work with pupils with SEN have been required to 'have regard to the *Code*'.

Every school should have a copy of the *Code of Practice*. The following is a very brief summary of some of the main points, together with the paragraph references in brackets for the location of the entire text.

### The principles of the *Code* (1:2)
These are:
- the needs of pupils with SEN must be addressed;
- there is a continuum of needs for which there should be a continuum of provision;
- children with SEN need access to a broad and balanced education including the National Curriculum;
- the needs of most pupils will be met in mainstream schools without a statement, and many children with statements will be educated in mainstream schools;
- young children may have SEN which require pre-school intervention by LEA and health services;
- partnership between parents, pupils, schools, LEAs and other agencies is important.

### The practices and procedures which support the principles (1:3)
These are:
- early identification and assessment;
- appropriate provision by the most appropriate agency, in most cases in the child's mainstream school without a statutory assessment;
- where assessments are needed, prescribed time limits and a requirement for more detailed statements;
- the child's wishes, in the light of their age and understanding, taken into account;
- close co-operation between the agencies concerned.

**The duties of the governing body (2:6)**

The governing body has overall responsibility for ensuring that provision is made for pupils with SEN. They are also required to report annually to parents on the school's special needs policy.

The governing body's report (2:11) must include information on the success of the policy; any changes in it; consultation with the LEA, the Funding Authority and other schools; and the allocation of resources for SEN over the year. The governing body must also 'have regard' to the *Code of Practice.*

**Roles and responsibilities in mainstream schools (2:7)**

The *Code* assigns responsibility to:

- the governing body (in co-operation with the headteacher): determining policy, establishing staffing and funding for SEN, maintaining an oversight of the school's work. They may appoint a governor or a committee to take a particular interest in SEN;
- the headteacher: responsibility for day-to-day management, informing the governing body and working with the SENCO;
- the SENCO: responsibility for the day-to-day operation of the school's SEN policy and for co-ordinating provision for pupils with SEN, especially at Stages 2 and 3;
- all teaching and non-teaching staff: involvement in developing the school's SEN policy; aware of procedures for identification, assessment and provision for pupils with SEN.

# The SENCO - an overview of the role

The responsibilities of the special educational needs co-ordinator, as set out in paragraph 2:14 of the *Code of Practice,* divide into the following areas:

- taking responsibility for the day-to-day operation of the school's SEN policy;
- liaising with and advising fellow teachers;
- co-ordinating provision for pupils with SEN;
- maintaining the school's SEN register and overseeing the records of all pupils with SEN;
- liaising with parents;
- contributing to staff in-service training (INSET);
- liaising with external agencies.

In reality this simple list covers a wide-ranging, time-consuming and frequently very stressful range of duties. These can include, in no particular priority order:

- negotiating with headteacher and governing body for appropriate resourcing;
- protecting support teaching time when threatened by the 'cover' rota;
- screening intakes and year groups;
- making diagnostic assessments for individual pupils;
- liaising with feeder schools and collating information from these for other staff;
- planning, managing and reviewing IEPs;
- working to involve a wide range of staff in IEPs;
- working with subject departments and curriculum co-ordinators on differentiation of the curriculum;
- devising forms and persuading staff to complete them;
- encouraging parents to be involved in assessment and review procedures;
- arranging reviews so that everyone can attend;
- providing a central point of contact and support for all those staff, both from within the school and outside, who work with pupils with SEN.

There are, I am sure, many more that SENCOs will add from their own experiences!

**Starting points**
When faced with this range of responsibilities, it is essential that the SENCO remembers two important points. Firstly, from paragraph 2:7 of the *Code*, 'Provision for pupils with special educational needs is a matter for the school as a whole'. The SENCO cannot work in isolation. A main consideration will be how to achieve this whole school approach. Secondly, careful thought needs to be given to how best to develop each of the SENCO's designated roles in the context of the school situation.

As the *Code of Practice* acknowledges in describing how schools might decide on their responses to its requirements, each school is unique.

The detail of what they decide to do may vary according to the size, organisation, location and pupil population of the school. The effect of their having regard to the *Code* is also likely to develop with time: much will depend upon schools' starting points.

*(Code of Practice,* 1994, Foreword, paragraph 7)

**Reviewing needs and resources**

In small schools it is frequently the headteacher who takes on the SENCO role and carries all the responsibilities listed above. In the largest secondary schools the SENCO may lead a small team of teachers who can share some of the responsibilities. Whatever the situation, it is important for the SENCO to review the precise extent of the role and the practical responsibilities involved in the light of the resources presently available, in terms of budget, time and personnel involved in working with SEN.

This review could form the basis of a presentation to senior management and/or governing body, clarifying the requirements of the *Code of Practice* in the context of the needs of the pupils in the school and the resourcing needed to meet them.

It may also be useful to draw up a list of priorities and establish a time scale for developing aspects of the SENCO role as described in the *Code of Practice*. This could also help to inform INSET needs, both for the SENCO and other staff.

# SEN policy

The *Code of Practice* in paragraph 2:10 sets out the requirements that the school's SEN policy should cover. The governing body has a statutory duty to see that a policy is produced and to report on its success in its annual report to parents.

In practice, the production of the policy will probably be devolved to the headteacher or SENCO, but the process should involve all the staff of the school, both teaching and non-teaching, and take account of the views of parents and outside agencies.

In brief, producing an effective policy may involve:
- looking at any existing SEN policy and reviewing it against the information required as set out in paragraph 2:10;
- consulting with teaching staff, non-teaching staff, parents and governors, possibly involving representatives of all of these in a working group, to draw up a draft policy;
- considering the policy alongside existing policies such as behaviour policies and arrangements for home-school liaison;

11

- identifying professional development needs;
- modifying the draft policy in the light of consultation with a wider group;
- presenting the policy to the governing body for discussion and, if approved, for adoption;
- establishing a cycle of monitoring and review;
- deciding how the policy should be made available to parents.

The more the whole staff are consulted and involved in the process of policy development, the more likely the policy is to exist as a practical working document.

> The involvement of all staff and the feeling of ownership which this produces means that the process of developing the policy may be regarded as of equal, or even greater importance, than the final document.
>
> (Gordon and Smith, 1995)

## The SEN policy as practice

If the SEN policy is to be more than a paper exercise, the SENCO has a pivotal role to play. The three sections into which paragraph 2:10 of the *Code of Practice* divides the policy are useful as a basis of review of the school's present procedures and as a starting point from which to develop a policy agreed and understood by all who will be involved in its implementation.

## Section 1: basic information

Section 1 deals with basic information about the school's SEN policy.

### *Objectives*

- Are the objectives clear and reflective of the school's ethos with regard to pupils with SEN?
- Have they been agreed by all staff?
- Do they complement the objectives of other policies in place in the school?

### *Name of the SENCO or person responsible for SEN*

- Are teaching staff, other staff, governing body and parents aware of who this is?
- How should parents and outside agencies be informed?

*Arrangements for co-ordinating provision for SEN*
- As this is the responsibility of the SENCO, is the range of responsibilities clearly set out and understood by all staff?
- Do staff understand their responsibilities in connection with each of the five stages?

*Admission arrangements*
- Are the admission arrangements in line with the LEA and school's admission policy?
- If, perhaps because of the school's facilities, priority is given to pupils with SEN, is this stated both in the policy and the school brochure?

*SEN specialisms and special units*
- For those schools which have these, are the specialisms, facilities and resources described?
- Are integration arrangements to mainstream for those pupils in units clearly set out?

*Special facilities which increase access to the school*
- Are special facilities, e.g. ramps and handrails, and the degree of access they provide described?

**Section 2: identification, assessment and provision**
Section 2 deals with identification, assessment and provision for pupils with SEN.
*Allocation of resources*
- What resources are available, both for statemented and non-statemented pupils?
- How are resources allocated to pupils with statements?
- How are resources allocated to pupils with SEN who do not have statements?
- How are the resources used?
- How is the use of resources monitored?

*Identification and assessment*
- What criteria are used for placing pupils at Stages 1 to 3 on the SEN register?
- Does the school use tests to screen new intakes or year groups?
- Is use made of information from parents and other schools?
- Are National Curriculum levels used as an indicator?
- Which diagnostic tests are used, and who administers them?

### Access to the curriculum
- How is the curriculum differentiated for pupils with SEN?
- What other arrangements support curricular access?
- How do class and subject teachers plan, record and assess the progress of pupils with SEN?

### Integration
- What arrangements ensure educational entitlement and effective integration for all pupils with SEN?

### Complaints
- Does the policy set out a procedure for dealing with complaints?
- Does it make reference to the school's general policy and the LEA policy?

## Section 3: staffing and partnership
Section 3 covers information about staffing policies and partnership with bodies other than the school.

### SEN in-service training
- Which staff have a designated responsibility for SEN?
- Does the SENCO have a specialist qualification?
- Have the training needs of the SENCO been identified?
- Have all staff and the governing body received training related to the *Code of Practice*?
- Have the staff's training priorities in relation to SEN been identified?
- Is INSET for SEN identified within the school development plan?

### Use of support services and specialist teachers
- Are the services available and the use made of them clearly documented?
- Are parents and staff aware of the support available?

### Partnership with parents
- Does the school actively seek to secure effective partnership with parents of pupils with SEN?
- How is this achieved?
- What areas need to be addressed?

### Links with other schools
- How is information regarding pupils with SEN transferred between schools?
- Are there meetings between the transferring and receiving school SENCOs?

- Is the SENCO involved in liaison with other schools in the same local cluster?
- Are there links with local special schools?
- Is there integration of pupils from special to mainstream and vice versa?

*Links with health, social services, education welfare and other agencies*
- How are these services used?
- Are parents and staff aware of these services and what they offer?
- Has the school a list of relevant local voluntary groups?

Discussion of these questions in the context of a particular school, and trying to establish answers to the further questions that will develop from them, should help the policy to be seen as a working document. Schools will need to decide how best this process might be achieved and how all those involved can be consulted at every stage.

Many of the questions listed above are considered in more detail in the remainder of this book. Further, more detailed information on policy development can be found in the NASEN publications by Luton, 1995 (for primary schools) and Gordon/Smith, 1995 (for secondary schools).

# The five-stage model for provision for special educational needs

The *Code of Practice* suggests a five-stage model for assessment and provision for special needs. (Schools and LEAs may adopt different models, but in practice most seem to have adopted the five stages.) The school has responsibility for pupils at Stages 1 to 3, with LEA involvement at Stage 3, and the LEA and school share joint responsibility at Stages 4 and 5.

## Criteria for pupil assessment
In setting up the special needs register and in placing children at Stages 1 to 3, schools will need to establish their criteria and the SENCO will have an important role to play in developing any assessment procedures. At Stage 1 it may be decided to enter on the register any pupil about whom a class or subject teacher expresses a concern and for whom they are providing extra support within the classroom situation. However, as it is necessary to involve parents at this stage and to gather supporting information, schools

15

will need to decide what constitutes the normal support and differentiation provided for many pupils and which are the pupils about whom there is a level of concern which requires a more formal intervention.

Before moving pupils to Stage 2, the SENCO will need to be involved in reviewing progress at Stage 1 and in establishing if a move to Stage 2 is appropriate.

The transfer of pupils from Stage 2 to Stage 3 may vary in procedure depending on the LEA involved. In some LEAs, schools may use their own systems to decide that a pupil should be placed at Stage 3, referring to outside agencies for advice and support in drawing up more detailed IEPs. In others, the LEA acts as the 'gatekeeper' for Stage 3, providing criteria against which to measure the child's performance and with an assessment from the appropriate support service before agreeing that the child can be placed at this stage.

LEAs will also provide set criteria to decide whether a child should proceed to Stages 4 and 5. At these stages the records of interventions made by the school at the first stages become crucial.

### The SENCO's involvement in assessment
Before considering the stages in more detail, here is a summary of the possible SENCO involvement. (Further information relating to record keeping; IEPs; reviews; and liaison with colleagues, parents and outside agencies is included in the following chapters.)

At all stages the SENCO may be involved in:
- updating the special needs register;
- maintaining records for pupils with SEN;
- liaison with and advice to colleagues;
- liaison with parents;
- assessment of individual pupils;
- direct teaching input;
- contributing to in-service training.

### The SENCO's stage-by-stage tasks
*Stage 1*
- Assessment procedures, such as initial screening on entry to the school;
- discussing an initial concern with parents;

- gathering information about pupils' difficulties and needs;
- advice to colleagues regarding classroom-based strategies;
- contributing to the review process.

## Stage 2
- Reviewing information gathered at Stage 1;
- assessing present need;
- drawing up an IEP in consultation with teaching staff;
- involvement in monitoring and reviewing the IEP;
- discussion with parents and colleagues about the appropriate next step;
- considering referral to an external specialist for pupils to be moved to Stage 3.

## Stage 3
- Gathering information and completing paperwork for referral to outside agencies;
- liaison with outside agencies;
- drawing up the IEP in consultation with teacher and external specialist;
- liaison with parents;
- organising and attending review meetings.

## Stage 4
- Discussing the need to request statutory assessment with parents;
- gathering additional information from teaching staff;
- completing the initial referral form;
- co-ordinating visits of those contributing to the assessment process;
- contributing to the assessment process;
- liaising with parents and LEA officers;
- continued involvement in the IEP and liaison with teaching staff.

## Stage 5
- Drawing up an IEP using the targets set in the statement;
- monitoring the targets set;
- setting up the support provided as a result of the statement;
- liaising with the support assistant and/or support teacher;
- liaising with external support specialist, e.g. speech and physiotherapists;
- co-ordinating arrangements for annual review;
- drawing up the review report.

## Stage 1: classroom intervention

Much of the responsibility at Stage 1 lies with class and subject teachers. It is the teacher who is likely to raise initial concerns. At Stage 1 the response to these concerns is intervention in the normal classroom situation. The SENCO's role is to assist the teacher in gathering information regarding the pupil's difficulties, to provide advice and support to those who teach the child and to include the child's name on the school's special needs register.

### *Consulting parents*

This step will involve consultation with parents. Depending on the systems within the school, this responsibility may rest with the class teacher, headteacher or SENCO. Ideally, this consultation should be by personal contact. It should be kept as informal and low key as possible in order not to alarm the parent, and an explanation of the terms 'Stage 1' and 'special needs register', if used, may be needed.

If the school has prepared a leaflet relating to special needs, the parent may like to have a copy at this stage.

If the parents cannot be contacted personally and communication has to be by letter, this should be kept as simple as possible, offering the parent the opportunity to contact the school for further information. An example of a proforma for a letter expressing initial concern to parents is included in Appendix 1.

### Support at Stage 1

Support for the pupil at Stage 1 may include some of the following:
- differentiation - by teaching style
  by classroom organisation
  by learning outcomes
  by resources used
  by support and extension materials;
- direct support from the class teacher;
- peer tutoring;
- IT support;
- parental involvement, such as paired reading;
- support from a classroom assistant or voluntary helper.

### Record keeping at Stage 1

As the Stage 1 record is completed when the pupil is first placed on the special needs register, it can serve a dual purpose. As well as showing the major cause for concern and the action to be taken, it can also contain all the relevant personal details of the pupil which will then not need to be repeated on subsequent records. It is also worthwhile to record the pupil's strengths. This is useful in setting the difficulty in context and identifying positive areas on which to build, and can be particularly valuable when planning for pupils with behavioural difficulties.

Information required at Stage 1 includes that which is available from normal school records, including National Curriculum attainments, any results of standardised tests, reports on the child in the school setting and relevant information regarding behaviour and health or social problems. This need not involve a mammoth paper exercise. The Stage 1 record may just refer to where this information can be found.

### Parents' views

The views of parents should also be recorded, regarding the child's health and development, their perceptions of his or her performance, progress and behaviour, both at school and at home, and any other factors which may contribute to the child's difficulty. It is also useful to record their views on the action they feel is appropriate to help their child.

In the case of a young child, the teacher may have much of this information from their contact with the child's parents on entry to the school. In the case of an older pupil this information can be very useful when planning appropriate interventions.

The gathering of this information from parents will obviously need sensitive handling. It may, in some cases, be acquired over a period of time. Some parents may be happy to express their views in writing, while others may need personal support and encouragement.

Appendix 2 contains a proforma list of questions which can either be used as the basis of an informal interview with parents or adapted as a questionnaire which parents might complete. Some questions may need to be amended according to the age of the pupil and the SENCO's present knowledge. Supplementary questions may be needed in the light of the school situation or the pupil's personal circumstances. The completed form can then be appended to the Stage 1 Record Sheet and updated as necessary. Further information on working with parents is included in the sections relating to partnership with parents and review meetings.

*Pupils' views*

The views of the pupil should also be noted. Even at an early stage pupils' perceptions of their difficulty can provide a useful insight when considering methods of support but, once again, sensitivity and knowledge of the pupil will determine how best this information might be obtained.

The record should then briefly outline the strategies being used to support the pupil in the classroom situation.

**Review at Stage 1**

The arrangements to review progress at Stage 1, and the decision as to whether the pupil should continue on Stage 1, move to Stage 2, or be removed from the register will also need to be included in the record sheet. As this stage represents a low level of intervention, the recorded review details need only be quite brief. The review process itself will probably involve informal discussion between either class teacher or SENCO and parents.

At this stage, given the numbers of pupils who may be registered at Stage 1 and the time available, the review process should be simple and informal. The review could be built into the normal parents' evening, or at a time when the parent normally visits the school, or it could be by a telephone call to the parent. Schools will need to decide on their own protocols to ensure a consistency of approach and review within a reasonable time scale.

Whichever review method is chosen, the parent will want to know what progress has been made and the SENCO's opinion of what should happen next. The parent may have a contribution to make to the review by providing information about the work they have been doing at home with the child or giving their opinion as to which strategies have been most successful. For those parents who are difficult to contact, it may be necessary to send a letter inviting them to contact school and, if there is no response to this, informing them of the outcome of the review process.

An example of a Stage 1 Record Sheet is included in Appendix 7. Remember, it is only an example. It may need to be amended (or completely rewritten) to suit your school situation, but it will provide a starting point on which to base your own systems. You may wish to consider using a colour coding system for documentation at each of the five stages so that you and other staff can see at a glance which stage a pupil has reached.

## Stage 2: the SENCO's leading role

At Stage 2 the SENCO takes a more leading role, reviewing the information gathered at Stage 1, seeking additional information if necessary and making an assessment of the child's present needs. The SENCO will continue to liaise with parents and to offer advice and information to teaching colleagues regarding the child's difficulties and appropriate strategies and interventions. One of the main roles for the SENCO at this stage is to draw up an IEP in consultation with those who teach the child and, if possible, involving the parents.

## Support at Stage 2

Support at this stage builds on that provided at Stage 1 but may include access to:
• increased differentiation of the curriculum;
• additional or modified resources;
• working in a small group – within the class or withdrawn;
• individual teaching by the SENCO or other staff;
• support in the classroom from a teacher or classroom assistant;
• IT support.

## Review at Stage 2

The review of progress at Stage 2 will involve the SENCO and other staff involved in the delivery of the IEP together with the parents. It may take the form of a formal review meeting or discussion between professionals followed by an informal meeting or telephone call between the SENCO and parents. The method of review will depend on the systems in place in the school, the time available to the SENCO, the ease of contacting the parents and possibly the degree of concern at this stage. For a few parents it may be necessary to communicate the outcome of the review in writing, but this is obviously the least desirable method.

If the pupil's progress is still a cause for concern after two reviews, and if the school feels that the strategies so far employed are not meeting with success, then referral to an outside agency for additional support will need to be considered, together with the placement of the pupil at Stage 3 on the SEN register. Parents must be consulted before referral to an outside agency takes place. Whatever the form of the review, it will need to consider:
• pupil progress in relation to the targets set;
• the effectiveness of the IEP;

- any new and relevant information;
- parental contribution to the IEP;
- the views of the pupil;
- future action.

## Stage 3: referral to an outside agency

At Stage 3 the SENCO still takes the lead working closely with class and subject teachers. At this stage referral is made to an external agency in order to seek expert advice to input the IEP at Stage 3. If the referral is to an LEA agency such as a learning or behaviour support service, or to a psychological service, there is likely to be a standard referral form for the school to complete. This will need to be accompanied by evidence of the interventions used at Stage 1 and the IEPs and their reviews at Stage 2, together with any other relevant information, including the views of parents.

The assessment of the external specialist should enable them to contribute to the drawing up of the IEP and the setting of appropriate targets. Their level of involvement in the IEP should be recorded. It may, for example, involve direct involvement with the pupil on a regular basis, regular monitoring, or ongoing advice and support to the school. The individual education plan can follow a very similar format to that at Stage 2, but it is more likely that the activities and strategies used to implement the plan will involve direct support for the pupil, either individually or as part of a group. This support may be from the SENCO, a support teacher, a classroom support assistant or an external specialist.

## Review at Stage 3

Review meetings at Stage 3 will consider the same items as those at Stage 2, but are likely to be more formal meetings as they will involve input from an external agency and also the consideration of whether the pupil should be referred for statutory assessment, if there have been two or more reviews at Stage 3 and if the pupil is not considered to be making sufficient progress to remain at Stage 3, or should revert to Stage 2.

If a request for statutory assessment is considered necessary then the SENCO must consult with the parents and advise the headteacher of this. If the parents have not attended the review meeting, then they should be contacted personally before a request for statutory assessment is made.

**Stages 4 and 5: statutory assessment**
The procedures for statutory assessment and the issue of a statement of special educational needs are set out in paragraphs 3:1 to 4:80 of the *Code of Practice* in detail. LEAs should also have issued guidance and appropriate documentation to schools on the conduct of the process.

Referral for statutory assessment can come either from a formal request from a parent or from the school, usually following progress through Stages 1 to 3. In exceptional circumstances, for example sudden medical difficulties or the admission of a pupil from another school, schools can make referrals without these stages. If a referral is made by the school under normal circumstances, they will need to state clearly the reasons for referral and provide evidence including:
- records of interventions at Stages 1 to 3, including IEPs, with indication of teaching approaches, monitoring arrangements and outcomes;
- reviews of progress at Stage 1 to 3, including decisions made and outcomes;
- health checks and medical advice;
- involvement of outside agencies, and views of other professionals;
- views of parents, and pupils where appropriate, on Stages 1 to 3 and support strategies offered so far.

*The set time scale*
Following this referral the LEA should follow a set time scale outlined in paragraph 3:30 of the *Code of Practice*. In brief, the time scale for the LEA is as follows:

6 weeks      to consider whether a statutory assessment is necessary. Parents must be notified of this decision.
10 weeks     to make the assessment.
2 weeks      to draft the statement or the note in lieu.
8 weeks      to finalise the statement.

If the LEA decides to carry out a statutory assessment, written evidence will be requested from:
- school;
- parents;
- educational psychologist;
- health services;
- social services;
- other agencies, or others whose contribution is seen by LEA or parents as desirable.

*Parents' participation*

The LEA will inform the parents of the Named LEA Officer, who will act as a source of information for the parents within the LEA and will liaise on any arrangements relating to the statutory assessment and statement. The LEA will also identify a Named Person, in co-operation with the parents, who is independent of the LEA and can give the parents information and advice. If the request for statutory assessment has been made by the parents and the LEA makes the decision not to proceed with this, then the parents have the right to appeal to the SEN Tribunal against the decision (paragraph 3:96, *Code of Practice*). Similarly, if the decision of the LEA, following statutory assessment, is not to issue a statement, then the parents can again appeal to the tribunal (paragraph 4:17, *Code of Practice*).

## The SEN Tribunal

The *Education Act 1993* established the SEN Tribunal as a means for parents to appeal against LEA decisions relating to assessments and statements. The *Code of Practice* sets out the parents rights of appeal. In addition to the two areas described above, parents can also appeal if they disagree with parts 2, 3 or 4 of their child's statement, if the LEA refuses to reassess their child or change the name of the school in the statement, or against an LEA decision to cease to maintain a statement.

The SEN Tribunal is an independent body which is based in London, but appeals are heard locally. The tribunal consists of three people, including the Chair who is a lawyer. The other members will have experience of special educational needs and local government. Parents can ask two professionals who know their child to speak on their behalf at the tribunal. Similarly the LEA will have professional representatives.

*How to appeal*

The DfE has produced a booklet, 'Special Educational Needs Tribunal: How to Appeal'. Although the target audience for this booklet is parents, it provides useful information on the procedures and timetable for the appeal. If a SENCO is asked by the LEA to appear at a tribunal, then the LEA will almost certainly provide support and guidance before the appeal. If a SENCO is asked by a parent to take part in a tribunal appeal, it would still be useful for them to contact their LEA to inform them and to request advice.

**Note in lieu**
Not all statutory assessments result in a statement of special educational needs. The LEA may issue a 'note in lieu of a statement' setting out their reasons for not issuing a statement with supporting evidence from the statutory assessment. All the evidence collected during the assessment is forwarded to the parents and, with their agreement, to the school. The intention is that this information will be used by those working with the child in planning appropriate interventions using the resources already available in school. Information relating to notes in lieu is included in paragraphs 4:17 to 4:23 of the *Code of Practice.*

**A statement issued**
If a statement is issued it will be set out as follows:
- Part 1, Introduction, will set out the child's personal details.
- Part 2, Special educational needs, will describe the child's SEN as identified from the assessment.
- Part 3, Special educational provision, will set out the educational objectives, provision to meet the objectives and monitoring arrangements.
- Part 4, Placement, will name the school or specify provision other than at a school.
- Part 5, Non-educational needs, will give details of the child's other needs, e.g. health, for which provision is needed.
- Part 6, Non-educational provision, will set out the arrangements to meet these needs.

Part 3 of the statement will be the section on which the SENCO, working with all other teaching and non-teaching staff involved, will base the pupil's IEP at this stage. This may also involve working with staff from a specialist support service if an input of this type is specified in the statement.

If the statement specifies a cash amount, the SENCO, in consultation with the headteacher, will need to decide how this resource should be used in order to ensure that the recommendations of Part 3 of the statement are met. Evidence will be needed to show how the money has been spent, together with records monitoring the effectiveness of the provision.

The LEA must ensure that the statement is reviewed within twelve months. Further information on the procedures for annual reviews is included in the chapter entitled Review meetings.

# Record keeping and documentation

The starting point here is the existing system for recording the SENCO's involvement with pupils with SEN. If there is an effective system, that works and that fits in with the recommendations of the *Code of Practice* and with the requirements of the particular LEA, then it is best to stick with it. At least the SENCO can look at the present systems as a baseline to see what can stay intact and what will need revision. Many schools have very effective systems which cover many of the requirements, particularly for Stage 1, and there is no need to duplicate these.

The SENCO will, however, need to be able to produce evidence of interventions at Stages 1 and 2 if it is decided that it is necessary to refer a pupil to an outside agency for their involvement at Stage 3. For that reason, it is probably useful to have at least a simple record to show where the more detailed information is located.

## Designing a manageable system

Each SENCO will also need to decide how to maintain a balance between the information that needs to be recorded and establishing a manageable system which will not be too onerous for the SENCO or colleagues, and that will not involve information being repeated. In designing a system, these are useful points to remember:

- Keep it simple.
- Avoid repetition of information recorded elsewhere.
- Ensure all the necessary information can be recorded and dated.
- Check with the LEA to see if they have guidance or proformas to offer.
- Consult with colleagues; they will be using it too.
- Have a trial period before adopting any new system formally.
- Be prepared to revise and review.

## The records needed

The records needed will include the special register and individual records for pupils at each of the five stages. From Stage 2 onwards the records will need to include an IEP. For Stages 3, 4 and 5 the school will also need to use LEA documentation for any referral to a specialist service, request for statutory assessment, contribution to assessment and annual review for pupils at Stage 5.

**The special needs register**

All that is necessary here is a fairly simple document to provide an overview of the numbers of pupils with special needs in the school, together with the reasons for their inclusion on the register and the stage at which they are placed. This will enable the register to be easily kept up to date. It may also be useful to completely update it on an annual basis at the start of the new school year.

This easily accessible document provides an overview of special needs within the school, giving information on:
• the total number of pupils with SEN in the school;
• the numbers of pupils at each stage;
• the categories of need for which the school is providing.

This information should assist the SENCO, contributing information to inform the school development plan and review of the SEN policy.

A possible format for a register is included in Appendix 6.

# Identification and assessment

In setting out the detail that should be included in the school's SEN policy, the *Code of Practice* refers to identification and assessment arrangements for pupils with SEN. This process of identification and assessment should be seen as part of the cycle of assessment, planning and review which underpins all teaching. While identification and assessment are obviously linked, it is probably useful to consider each separately.

**Identification of special needs**

Early identification of a pupil's special educational needs is essential if effective provision is to be made. The school could consider how pupils with SEN are identified now and when the process of identification begins. Before pupils enter school, is information gathered from:
• parents?
• feeder schools?
• outside agencies?

Does this information include:
- SATs results?
- scores in standardised test?
- medical information?
- information relating to behaviour and social difficulties?

How is the information used?
- Is relevant information conveyed to all staff who teach pupils with SEN?
- How is this communication achieved?
- How do staff use the information they receive?

Following intake:
- Is there a screening process for the whole year group?
- What systems are in place to record concerns expressed by staff and others?
- How is this information followed up?
- What criteria are used to decide which pupils will be placed on the SEN register at Stage 1?

## Having structures in place

It is important that schools have structures in place which ensure that pupils' needs and difficulties are identified in order that appropriate interventions can be put into place. Much of this process can be built into the school's usual intake procedures for liaison with parents and feeder schools, but it is essential that if a pupil is identified as having SEN all appropriate information is gathered and communicated to those who will teach him or her. However, some pupils may be identified as having special needs only after they are in school, and the information gathering process will begin in the school context.

## First registering concern

Identification of pupils already in school will probably be triggered by a class or subject teacher. In larger schools, and particularly secondary schools where a pupil will be taught by several members of staff, it may be useful to develop a form on which staff can register these concerns. This will enable the SENCO to be aware if a pupil is experiencing a difficulty in just one area or across a range of subjects or activities, and to have access to a range of professional opinions. (An example of a proforma for expressing concern is included in Appendix 1.) This can be particularly useful for pupils with emotional and behavioural difficulties where problem behaviours may be seen in some areas and not others, and where this information can help to inform intervention strategies.

Some schools may prefer to use pastoral or curriculum meetings to raise initial concerns and decide whether the pupil should be considered for inclusion on the SEN register. In primary schools the process may be an informal conversation between SENCO and class teacher, but the concern should be recorded if it is to lead to the pupil being entered on the SEN register and parents contacted.

Whichever systems of identification a school has in place, consideration will need to be given to what constitutes criteria for inclusion on the SEN register at Stage 1 in order that there is a consistency of approach, understood by all staff, as to what constitutes a special need. While Stage 1 is largely the responsibility of the class or subject teacher, the SENCO is involved in advice, liaison and record keeping and in informing the parents, so it is essential that this early stage of intervention is appropriately managed.

### Assessment of pupils
In considering assessment, the term needs to be set in context. Assessment includes ongoing formative teacher assessment of all pupils, summative assessment using end of Key Stage tasks and tests, examinations and, for pupils with SEN, diagnostic assessment to inform planning and assessment as part of the process of statutory assessment. In some LEAs assessments of year groups of pupils, using standardised test, are part of the process of allocating delegated non-statutory funding for special educational needs.

The SENCO's role in assessment for individual pupils is likely to focus on two areas, diagnostic assessment to inform future planning, and assessment as part of the process leading to statutory assessment.

### Gathering the first information
The initial process of gathering information should help to identify those pupils who have SEN and to clarify what those needs are. Ongoing assessment and review is needed to inform future planning. This assessment process should build on systems already in place in school. In their planning class and subject teachers build in assessment opportunities and these provide valuable information to direct teaching, particularly in differentiating the curriculum at Stages 1 and 2. Information from teacher assessments may also be useful in planning targets for IEPs.

### More detailed information
For some pupils a more focused individual assessment may be necessary if more detailed information is needed, for example in relation to a pupil's

difficulties in acquiring literacy skills, or in informing planning for pupils with behavioural difficulties. The form that the assessment takes will depend on the needs of the pupil so far identified, but will need to address the following questions:

- What is the assessment hoping to achieve?
- Are its outcomes likely to be useful in planning for this pupil?
- Will it enable the pupil to show what he or she can do, as well as where he or she is failing?
- Has all the information available about this pupil been considered?
- Who will be involved in the assessment process: class teacher, SENCO, others?
- Will the assessment involve a classroom observation to focus on the pupil's learning style, level of concentration, and peer relationships?
- Which diagnostic tests are appropriate?

Consideration of these questions with the needs of a particular pupil in mind should help to identify which form of assessment, or which diagnostic test might be most appropriate.

**Planning targets**
The information gathered from any assessment will need to be set in the wider context of knowledge of the pupil from staff and parents. If the SENCO has been involved in a classroom observation or a one-to-one diagnostic assessment, both of which are time consuming, it is obviously essential that the information gathered is carefully used and shared with others as appropriate. From the assessment the SENCO should be able to work with teaching staff in planning appropriate interventions, including targets for an IEP.

The assessment should not be seen only as a means of providing a baseline and targets for the pupil, but as a means of providing teaching staff with more general information relating to the pupil's learning style, concentration span and behaviour which can be valuable in overall classroom management of the pupil's needs.

**Statutory assessment**
Details of assessments and their impact on IEPs will also be needed as part of the information required by the LEA to support a request for statutory assessment. Some LEAs provide guidelines as to the criteria for statutory assessment relating to literacy, numeracy and specific learning difficulties

(dyslexia). These criteria may include reference to particular standardised tests and to centile scores which might indicate that a request for statutory assessment would be considered. It is obviously important for a SENCO to be aware of these criteria and of the relevant tests.

### Useful diagnostic resources

A list of tests and resources which may be useful in assessment and planning are included in the References, further reading and resources in the back of this book. The list is not comprehensive, but could provide a starting point for the bank of materials which a SENCO may develop over a period of time, the detail of which will depend on the phase in which he or she is working.

It will also be useful for the SENCO to consult with other SENCOs and specialist teachers, such as those employed by LEA support services, as to which diagnostic resources they find most useful. This can help to avoid the purchase of costly mistakes, as testing is only worthwhile it if provides useful outcomes. Assessment may also be an area which a newly appointed SENCO may identify for professional development.


# The individual education plan

Paragraph 2:93 of the *Code of Practice* gives the detail of what should be included in an IEP and the way in which it should be drawn up. It recommends that the plan should build on the child's present curriculum and make use of materials and resources readily available to those who teach the child. It also recommends close liaison between those who teach the child, and that the plan should be implemented, at least in part, in the normal classroom situation. The content of the plan should include reference to:
• the nature of the child's learning difficulties;
• action - special educational provision;
• staff involved, including frequency of support;
• specific programmes, activities, material, equipment;
• help from parents at home;
• targets to be achieved in a given time;
• any pastoral care or medical requirements;
• monitoring and assessment arrangements;
• review arrangements and date.

**The pupil's present needs**
In drawing up an IEP the first step will be to make an assessment of the pupil's present needs. This will involve at least some of the following:

- reviewing the success of interventions at Stage 1;
- further diagnostic assessment;
- gathering information about curriculum progress from other staff;
- classroom observation;
- discussion with parents;
- considering the pupil's views and strengths.

From this assessment of needs the teaching priorities can be established, along with the pupil's present skills in these areas. This will establish a baseline from which to work on developing the targets or objectives to be achieved within a given time. Although these targets will need to be specific if they are to have outcomes against which performance can be monitored and measured, they also need to be seen in the context of the pupil's access to the whole curriculum and general development. Concentration on skills-based targets should not ignore the pupil's need for support in curricular areas while these and other targets are being achieved.

**Involving the pupil**
Two further considerations are involving the pupil in the drawing up and reviewing of the plan, and deciding on a manageable number of targets. The *Code of Practice* emphasises the involvement of pupils in implementing IEPs. As the *Code* states,

> Young people are more likely to respond positively to intervention programmes if they fully understand the rationale for their involvement and if they are given some responsibility for their own progress ...

> Involving children in tracking their own progress within a programme designed to meet their particular learning or behaviour difficulty can greatly contribute to an improved self-image and greater self-confidence.
> (paragraph 2:36)

In deciding the number of targets to be included in an IEP, particularly at Stages 2 and 3, it is important to consider what is a reasonable number to manage within the context of the school and the resources available. Three or four targets are likely to be the maximum which can be managed effectively, and these may include, as well as skills-based targets, ones which are social or cross-curricular.

## Writing targets

The first consideration will be to decide what the priority areas are. Whatever targets are set will need to be firmly based on the pupil's present achievements and will need to be 'smart':

Specific
Measurable
Attainable
Realistic
Time limited.

### Specific targets

Make them precise and firmly related to the pupil's present achievements. Write them as positive outcomes, e.g. 'Jo will successfully read the ten key words listed on five separate occasions'.

### Measurable targets

Establish exactly what the success criteria are for the pupil to have achieved the target, e.g. correctly spell five words containing the 'ch' digraph on four separate occasions.

### Attainable targets

Make sure the target is within the pupil's grasp. 'Read fluently by the end of the year' is likely to evade many pupils! Base the target on the pupil's present achievements and limit the number of targets. Three or four are the most that are likely to be manageable either by the pupil or the staff involved.

### Relevant targets

Identify as targets those skills which are essential for the child to master and which will enable improved access to the curriculum. If possible, involve the pupil in identifying priorities, especially at the secondary level.

### Time-limited targets

When setting targets consider the date that has been set to review the IEP. Be realistic about what the pupil is likely to be able to achieve in that period of time. Better to review the targets too frequently than to set targets which linger over extended periods of time. IEPs should be reviewed at least termly, but for some pupils more frequent review may be desirable.

Having decided on the targets, or the 'What?' of the plan, these questions then need to be addressed: How? Who? When? and Where?

## How?
How is the target to be achieved?
What activities will be involved?
What resources will be needed?

## Who?
Who is going to be involved in the activities?
Class/subject teachers?
SENCO?
Support teacher?
Support assistant?
Parent?

## When?
How often will the pupil have access to this support, and at what times?

## Where?
Will the support be in the classroom situation, or in a withdrawal session?

Monitoring and recording systems will also need to be considered.

### Communicating the content of IEPs
The SENCO will need to decide who should be informed of the content of the individual education plan. This could involve several people:
- pupil;
- class teacher;
- subject teacher;
- support teacher;
- classroom assistant;
- headteacher/senior management;
- parents;
- outside agencies.

It is useful for those involved in the delivery of the IEP, including the pupil, to sign it. This can indicate to pupil and parents a positive agreement between all those working together.

**Involving parents in targets**

If possible, actively involve parents in IEP targets. Some targets could be specific to the home situation, while in others the parents could provide additional support and reinforcement for activities being presented in school.

If the parents cannot be actively involved, it is still important to communicate the content of the IEP so that they are informed of the areas of need identified as priorities. If possible, ask one of the parents to sign the form as this will help to raise the status of the IEP in their, and their child's, eyes.

**The format of the IEP**

Keep the format as simple as possible, but make sure that it can be easily understood by all those who are involved in its delivery. Avoid repetition of information that is recorded elsewhere. Some detail relating to medical and pastoral arrangements may be recorded on the initial record sheets and there is no need to repeat these if they are still current. Cross-reference to other school records, e.g. pastoral and classroom records, if appropriate.

Three alternative formats are included in Appendix 9. One of them may work for your school, or you may wish to select some features from each.

**IEPs for pupils with emotional and behavioural difficulties**

Emotional and behavioural difficulties (EBD) are included in the *Code of Practice* under the general heading of Learning Difficulties. Individual education plans for pupils with these difficulties will need to be set within the context of the school's behaviour policy and reward systems. Before drawing up an IEP:

- list the problem behaviour(s);
- try to establish what triggers these behaviours;
- establish which is the priority difficulty;
- list the pupil's strengths;
- work with all those involved – pupil, teachers, parents – to decide on short-term objectives;
- write the objectives as positive outcomes, with no ambiguity;
- decide on success criteria;
- decide on recording and reward systems;
- monitor frequently and feed back to pupil;
- review targets regularly;
- consider how to involve pupils as fully as possible in both the setting of targets and their review.

## IEPs in secondary schools

The setting up of IEPs in secondary schools can cause difficulties in relation to communication, consistency and paperwork. Each school will have an individual response which will depend on the size of the school, amount of time available to the SENCO for liaison and record keeping, and the school's existing recording systems, both pastoral and curricular.

It is worthwhile to spend some time considering and discussing with subject departments the following points:

- Is there a named contact or link teacher for SEN in each department?
- How do subject departments plan for pupils with SEN and record their progress?
- How are the IEP targets decided: by SENCO, or by discussion with teaching staff?
- Are the IEP targets literacy/numeracy/behavioural or subject specific?
- Can targets be addressed in the subject curricular areas?
- How can the IEP content be communicated to each department?
- What will departmental input be and how will it be recorded?
- How will the paperwork of communication be managed?

There are no easy answers to these questions. The identification of a 'link' person in each department will certainly ease the process of communication, but it will fall to the SENCO to co-ordinate the management of the IEP and to gather and review the outcomes. An example proforma for an IEP for a secondary school is included in Appendix 10 as a basis from which to develop a school-specific model based on responses to the questions posed above.

## Involvement of the secondary-level pupil

An essential element of the IEP in a secondary school is the involvement of the pupil in both the setting and review of targets. If the pupil feels that his or her opinion on the way in which targets are approached is valued, then there is likely to be a more positive approach to the activities and hence a more successful outcome. Involvement in the review process is also helpful in enhancing self-esteem, encouraging the development of self-assessment and increasing motivation towards future targets.

More detailed information on IEPs can be found in the NASEN publication, 'Implementing the *Code of Practice:* Individual Education Plans' by Stella Warin.

# Classroom-based support for pupils with special educational needs

Some SENCOs, and it may be a fortunate few, have time on their timetable in which to work in the classroom alongside colleagues in order to support pupils with SEN. Whether support is provided in this direct way, or indirectly, careful consideration needs to be given as to how to provide the maximum support for pupils from the available resources.

## Allocating direct support

Deciding where to allocate direct support from a teacher or classroom assistant, if this is an available option, will involve looking at:

- the needs of individual pupils;
- pupil groupings;
- the demands of the curricular areas.

For direct support to be most effective, those doing the supporting need to have a clear understanding of:

- the aim of the lesson;
- the way in which the lesson content will be presented;
- the needs of the pupil(s) to be supported;
- the content of IEPs;
- available modified resources and support materials for the lesson.

If time for liaison with the class teacher is difficult to find, it can be very helpful for the teacher to photocopy the lesson plan and add any additional notes which the colleague providing support may find useful. Following the lesson, the support teacher or classroom assistant ideally needs an opportunity to feed back to the class or subject teacher and to discuss plans for the next lesson.

Support teachers can also be more directly involved in the presentation of the lesson by:

- team teaching;
- taking part of the lesson while the class or subject teacher provides the support;
- working with a group of pupils including those being directly supported.

**Indirect support for pupils**

Indirect support for pupils which can be provided by the SENCO or other support teachers includes:

- assisting class teachers and departments in planning for differentiation;
- preparation of resources and support material;
- developing a bank of suitable texts for use in research and project activities;
- providing support for recording techniques, such as tape recorders and word processing;
- providing follow-up support for pupils during withdrawal sessions.

# Liaison with colleagues

In order for the SENCO to be able to work effectively with colleagues, all staff of the school will need to have a clear understanding of their own responsibilities in supporting pupils with special educational needs, together with those of the SENCO, the headteacher and governing body. Some staff may not have a clear knowledge of the five-stage model outlined in the *Code of Practice* and, if this is the case, this could be a priority for an INSET session. Having established the responsibilities of staff at each stage, it is essential that all staff have access to appropriate information. The communication of information is a key responsibility of the SENCO.

**Communication of information**

The SENCO will need to decide what information it is relevant for staff to receive and who should have access to this. As well as class and subject teachers, some of the information may be necessary to inform the work of:

- classroom assistants;
- voluntary helpers in the classroom;
- other school staff such as lunchtime supervisors.

All those receiving information will need to understand its confidential nature.

The information provided to teaching staff needs to be presented in a way which will support their teaching. They will need to know:

- the nature of the pupil's difficulties;
- how these difficulties affect his or her classroom performance;
- which particular strategies will support the pupil best;

- what are the pupil's strengths and interests;
- what support, if any, the pupil is to receive from the SENCO or other adult;
- the targets for the present IEP if the pupil is at Stage 2 or above;
- any relevant personal or medical details.

How this information is communicated will depend on the size of the school and the numbers of pupils involved. If it is communicated on paper it will need to be concise and to point the teacher to where more information can be obtained if necessary. In a primary school it might be communicated by a meeting between SENCO and class teacher at the start of a term or year. In secondary schools with large subject departments, as well as ensuring that information is transferred to the form tutor and staff with pastoral responsibility, such as the head of year, it is useful to consider establishing link teachers in each subject area or faculty.

**Link teachers**
In some secondary schools link teachers in subject departments are already well established. In some cases this role evolved following departmental input into working parties developing the school's SEN policy. The link teacher can be involved in some or all of the following:
- membership of a cross-curricular group developing whole school approaches to special needs related issues;
- regular meetings with the SENCO to receive information regarding pupils with SEN which is then communicated to departmental colleagues;
- informing and liaising with colleagues regarding contributions to IEPs;
- collecting information within the department regarding pupils who are a cause for concern;
- gathering information relating to the monitoring of IEPs;
- leading work on differentiation within the department;
- developing resources.

As well as distributing information, the SENCO will need to establish systems for gathering it. The information the SENCO will need from staff within the school includes:
- initial expressions of concern;
- strategies used to support pupils at Stage 1 and their effectiveness;
- the pupil's success in achieving targets set in IEPs;
- contributions for review meetings if the subject or class teacher is not attending;
- details of the pupil's response to work with support teachers and classroom assistants.

As with identification of difficulties, the SENCO and staff will need to decide how this information can be communicated so that concise, accessible records can be kept. As for an initial expression of concern, the school may decide to develop a simple proforma for staff to complete which can then be appended to the pupil's SEN records. In secondary schools in particular, where large numbers of staff can be involved, such a proforma can be very useful. An example which could be adapted for use across the stages is included in Appendix 11.

## Support teachers and classroom assistants

As well as liaison with the school's teaching staff, the SENCO has an important role to play in working with other professionals such as visiting support teachers and classroom assistants working with statemented pupils. In working with these staff, who may only be in school for a small part of the week and who may not be employed directly by the school, consideration of the following points may be useful in establishing good relationships and the most effective support for pupils:

- ensure that staff have a complete timetable and general information such as a staff list, holiday dates, etc.;
- clarify marking, recording and communication systems used in school;
- give staff a clear understanding of their role and responsibilities in the school;
- make them feel their contribution is valued;
- provide them with feedback and support;
- involve them in evaluating/reviewing pupil progress;
- if possible, provide opportunities for them to participate in school-based INSET.

## The SENCO as 'expert'

As well as distributing and receiving information, the SENCO has an identified role in advising fellow staff. This implies that the SENCO is the school's SEN 'expert'. While this is undoubtedly the case in many schools, in some the SENCO is a newly identified role following the recommendations of the *Code of Practice* and the teacher appointed has little or no professional training for the post. In these situations this professional development should be identified by the school as a priority. In the interim, the SENCO may have to rely on informal support from other SENCOs, the LEA's support services and the membership of special needs associations to support their role.

In order to develop this advisory and liaison role, it is necessary for the SENCO to have time to meet with other staff both individually and as groups. An individuals staff may want to share the individual difficulties of particular pupils, to discuss strategies that have been used or to ask for extra support. Groups such as departmental staff may wish to involve the SENCO in discussions relating to curriculum differentiation, development of resources and classroom management issues. The SENCO may need to advise staff on pupils with physical or medical problems, or to discuss whole school approaches to behaviour management.

There will be situations when the SENCO will need to look outside the school in order to respond to a request for advice from a colleague. There will also be times when the SENCO will need to be a good listener for staff who need to 'let off steam' before being able to discuss a pupil's future needs!

## Managing resources for special needs

In managing resources for SEN, the SENCO will need to work with the governing body and headteacher to define exactly what the available resources are and how much, or little, of the management responsibility for these lies with the SENCO. In some small schools the headteacher and SENCO are one and the same person, the budget is very small and the management of resources is limited because of this. In large primary and most secondary schools the situation is more complex and schools will need to consider carefully how best resources should be managed and by whom. Resources can be divided into four areas:
- budget;
- time;
- human resources;
- material resources.

### The budget
The *Code of Practice* requires that the SEN policy should specify 'the allocation of resources to and amongst pupils with SEN' (paragraph 2:10, The school's SEN policy). This will represent a forward step for some SENCOs who in the past may have been unsure exactly how much money was in the school's budget for SEN. This uncertainty was sometimes caused by part of the non-statutory funding being included in the age-weighted

pupil unit and not clearly identified. Now that resourcing has to be specified, SENCOs should know how much is available and have a real part in negotiating for its most effective use. In local authorities where funding for special needs is fully delegated to schools, the SENCO will find the process of identification more simple, although the management issue may be increased when all external advice and support has to be bought in.

The SENCO should be aware of:
- the amount of funding for non-statutory SEN. In some authorities this resource is allocated on the basis of a proxy indicator such as free school meals. In others year groups are screened using a standardised test and the funding allocated on the basis of the results;
- the amount of funding for pupils with statements. In LEAs where this funding is still centrally held, this resource may be allocated as a number of teaching or support assistant hours. In others a sum of money will be allocated from which the SENCO will have to meet the needs identified in the statement;
- the allocation that the school makes from its own budget, for example for books and consumable resources;
- the amount the school has identified for professional development and INSET relating to special needs issues;
- how special need is identified within the school development plan.

The SENCO will need to be able to answer the following questions:
- Who will be responsible for managing the total budget?
- What does the budget have to cover?
- Is the school able to plan ahead to develop strategies and resources?
- How will support for pupils with statements be planned and managed?
- Will support be in-class, withdrawal groups or a combination of these?
- How will its effectiveness be monitored?
- How will the non-statutory funding be used?

SEN funding could be used for some of the following:
- to purchase additional teaching time for pupils with SEN;
- to buy time for a classroom support assistant to work at the direction of the SENCO or class teacher;
- to buy assessment, advice and support from outside agencies;
- to cover the timetable of the SENCO to allow him or her:
  to work with individuals and small groups of pupils;
  to support pupils in the classroom;

42

to attend review meetings;
to use diagnostic assessment materials with individual pupils;
to liaise with class/subject teachers to develop support strategies;
to complete administrative tasks such as referrals, review reports and records;
to develop materials and resources.

However the budget is spend, the school is accountable for its use. Those involved in monitoring the use of the budget will include the governing body, the local authority and Ofsted as part of the inspection process.

## Time

The school will have to make decisions regarding the amount of time available to the SENCO to carry out the various parts of the role. Some of these have been identified in the above section relating to budget, as time and money are obviously closely linked. There are obvious financial implications in allowing the SENCO time to work with individuals and small groups of pupils rather than teaching a whole class. Similarly, using diagnostic assessment materials to inform future teaching and planning of IEPs takes time from the teaching day.

Consideration of the grouping of pupils can also relate to the management of time as a resource. In some schools, particularly secondary, pupils with special needs are 'clustered' in teaching groups so that additional support can be used most effectively. This arrangement needs to be considered in the context of the school's other arrangements for grouping pupils and of the times when the group might not be directly supported and the burden that this might place on teaching staff. Similarly, the teaching support allocated to statemented pupils can often benefit pupils without statements who work with them either in the classroom or in withdrawal groups. A good knowledge of the needs of pupils before they enter the school and time to work with those who organise the timetable is essential if the SENCO is to be able to use the time resource with maximum efficiency.

Other parts of the SENCO role often depend on the goodwill of the SENCO and other staff in giving freely of their own time. The following questions need to be asked, although there may not be ready answers.
• Will review meetings only be held outside the school day?
• When will the SENCO and class/subject teachers liaise about classroom support at Stage 1?

- When will the SENCO and staff work together to develop IEPs?
- When will the SENCO liaise with and direct staff working with statemented pupils?
- When will the SENCO update records and write reports?
- When will liaison with outside agencies take place?
- When will the SENCO be available to meet parents?

In trying to establish acceptable answers to these questions, the school could look at its use of:
- directed time. Is there any to spare?
- staff meetings. Is SEN on the agenda on a regular basis?
- curricular/departmental meetings. Is there an opportunity for the SENCO to have an input to these?
- training days. Has SEN been identified as an area to be developed during these?

### Human resources
The human resources that the SENCO may be required to manage could be quite considerable, depending on the size of the school. As well as school staff working with pupils with special needs, it could include:
- specialist support teachers provided by outside agencies;
- classroom assistants;
- student teachers;
- voluntary helpers such as parents.

Many of the above, as well as working with pupils with SEN, will be working in the classroom alongside other teachers. For this reason it is useful for the SENCO, perhaps working with other staff, to develop guidelines for those working with pupils with SEN. These should complement any guidelines already in place in school for voluntary helpers or others working in school.

Preparation of such guidelines would need to include information regarding:
- general school systems and organisation;
- pastoral systems;
- school policies, e.g. behaviour, parent partnership and school visits;
- planning and recording systems in use in the class;
- roles and responsibilities in the classroom;
- IEPs, including monitoring and review arrangements;
- issues associated with confidentiality.

The management of the people who work with pupils with SEN cannot be separated from the budget and time management, but it also requires from the SENCO, on occasions, the skills of tact and diplomacy. The SENCO, in organising in-class support for pupils, will need to consider both the support staff involved and the teacher of the whole class or group as some teachers still find it difficult to have other staff working in 'their' classroom. Guidelines which clarify roles and responsibilities should help, as should time for the SENCO to be involved in setting up the support and involving the class teacher in the arrangements at every stage.

The timetable for support will have to take account of the needs of individual pupils and their placement within groups so that the maximum use is made of support staff without an overlap which involves several people supporting the same group. Where support staff, perhaps from outside the school, are allocated to statemented pupils, the issues of flexibility and balance will need to be addressed.

It may not be realistic or practical to have a different support teacher or classroom assistant for each statemented pupil, but equally if staff hours are allocated or bought in a block it may be difficult to match the times when the staff are available in school to the particular needs of individual pupils in relation to the timetable. A balance will need to be sought which establishes a match between the needs of the pupils, timetable and staff.

This balance should also help to secure a consistency in support staff which will enable them to have a clear understanding of the school ethos and systems. It will also enable the SENCO to build up relationships, offer appropriate advice and support, and allow the support staff to feel a part of the school. This balance can sometimes be difficult if the support teacher or classroom assistant is allocated from central funding and is line managed by, for example, a support service.

## Material resources
In developing a bank of resources within the school, the SENCO may first need to audit what is presently available.
- Is there a stock of resources for the development of basic literacy and numeracy skills?
- Are they age-appropriate for the pupils in the school?
- Do staff know where they are located?

- Are there resources available to support pupils with special needs across the curriculum?
- Are these resources housed centrally or with subject departments or curriculum co-ordinators?

In identifying these gaps in resourcing and in establishing priorities the SENCO will need to consult with class teachers and subject staff. Decisions as to how the development of resources should be funded may involve the headteacher and heads of subject departments. In developing subject specific resources it may be that part of a subject department's capitation may be directed to this, or it may be that the SENCO is allocated capitation in order to fulfil this role in consultation with colleagues.

Whatever system for developing resources is established, the SENCO should try to:
- work with colleagues to develop curriculum-based resources;
- build on existing good practice and established systems;
- catalogue existing resources and circulate this information to other staff as appropriate;
- keep colleagues informed of new resources which have been bought or developed within school. It may be necessary to provide some informal INSET on how to use and/or get the best from new resources;
- review the effectiveness of resources with colleagues and support staff;
- share ideas and information with SENCOs in other schools.

# Review meetings

Review meetings can be divided into those which cover Annual Reviews of statements of special educational needs and those which review the school-based stages. The *Code of Practice* requires that progress should be reviewed at all stages, that the effectiveness of present support should be considered and that future action should be planned.

### Stages 1 and 2: involving parents
At Stages 1 and 2, as has been previously mentioned, the *Code* does not state that a 'meeting' should be held. At Stage 1, paragraph 2:81 states that a review date should be set and that 'this might be within a term', and that the parents should be informed of this date. As has been stated earlier, this

review might be a discussion with a parent at a parents' evening and this is supported by the *Code* in paragraph 2:84, which also acts as a reminder of the necessity to inform parents of the outcome of any review procedure, particularly if the child is to be moved to Stage 2.

At Stage 2, there is similarly no prescribed method of review, but parents should be invited to contribute and should always be informed of the outcome (paragraph 2:98). The parental contribution to the review process at Stage 2 is particularly important if the parent has been involved in delivery of the IEP. At both Stages 1 and 2 the method of review will need to be decided in the context of the school's regular procedures for meeting with parents. If consideration is to be given to a child moving from Stage 2 to Stage 3, it will obviously be important to talk to the parents in person if at all possible.

### Stage 3: more formality
At Stage 3, the *Code of Practice* states in paragraph 2:113, 'the SEN co-ordinator should convene Stage 3 review meetings', continuing in paragraph 2:116, 'Parents should always be invited to and encouraged to attend Stage 3 reviews'. As stated earlier, as Stage 3 involves considering the views of external specialists and may be the precursor to a request for statutory assessment, there is a necessity for a more formal meeting to consider the child's future needs.

### Annual Reviews of statements
The LEA has a statutory requirement to review a statement annually and Section 6 of the *Code of Practice* sets out in detail the arrangements for Annual Reviews. This section also refers to the Transition Plan, to be drawn up at the first Annual Review after the young person's 14th birthday, and to the involvement of social services departments and careers services in reviews post-14.

The procedure for Annual Reviews, other than the transitional review, is as follows:
- The LEA initiates the review by writing to the headteacher.
- The headteacher: convenes the meeting;
  invites a representative of the LEA;
  invites the child's parents;
  invites the SENCO, class teacher or other staff as appropriate;
  invites other agencies as appropriate;

requests written advice from those invited;
circulates the advice two weeks before the meeting;
chairs the meeting;
prepares the review report.

In many instances much of this work will be carried out by the SENCO, including the chairing of the meeting in many schools. The meeting will need to address the following issues:

- the parents' view of the child's progress over the past year and their hopes for the future;
- the pupil's view of his or her progress over the past year and hopes for the future;
- the school's view of the pupil's overall progress during the year and progress towards the targets of the statement;
- any changes in the pupil's circumstances which affect his or her development and progress;
- if the present provision, including the National Curriculum or alternative provision, is appropriate;
- future targets against which progress will be assessed at the next review;
- any further action needed, and if so by whom;
- whether the present statement is appropriate;
- amendments needed to the statement, or recommendations that the LEA should cease to maintain the statement.

The review report: summarises the outcomes of the meeting;
sets new targets;
is circulated to all concerned;
is submitted to the LEA.

### The transitional review
For the first Annual Review following the young person's fourteenth birthday, also referred to as the transitional review, there are some differences to the above procedures:

- the LEA convenes the review meeting and invites those involved;
- the LEA ensures that other agencies such as social services are informed of the review and invited to attend;
- the LEA invites a representative from the careers service;
- following the review the LEA prepares the review report and the Transition Plan.

**The Transition Plan**
The Transition Plan draws together information from the school and from other agencies who are likely to be involved in the young person's transition to adult life. In drawing up the plan, consideration is given to the views of the school, professionals, the family and the young person. A series of questions which the Transition Plan should address is set out in the *Code of Practice* in paragraph 6:46, and the plan should cover all aspects of the young person's development and allocate responsibility for different aspects of development to specific agencies and professionals.

The involvement of social services at this stage is important if the young is disabled and may require services from the local authority after leaving school, or who because of significant special needs may need a multi-disciplinary assessment leading to a care plan which may involve the provision of further education facilities. This involvement by social services is detailed in paragraphs 6:48 to 6:52.

**Organising review meetings**
The organisation of review meetings can be divided into those activities which take place prior to the meeting, and which help to ensure that it will be effective and run smoothly, and the organisation and running of the meeting itself. The following guidelines may be helpful in considering both of these areas.

*Prior to the meeting*
- Decide who should be invited. Try not to overwhelm parents with more professionals than necessary.
- Agree the date with external specialists first. Their diaries often fill very quickly.
- Establish the agenda for the meeting, referring to the requirements of the appropriate stage of the *Code of Practice.*
- Issue the invitations, giving ample notification. In the invitations, include a copy of the agenda and indicate the length of time available for the meeting.
- Seek the views of the pupil, either directly or via the parents.
- Gather information from other school staff and external agencies not attending.
- Draw together this information in order to be able to report concisely to the meeting.
- Try to find a quiet and private room for the meeting.

**Inviting parents**

Although it is ideal if parents can be contacted personally or by telephone in order to invite them to reviews, it is also useful for them to have the arrangements in writing in order to be able to refer to them.

Parents will need to know:
- the purpose of the meeting;
- the time and place, and the length of the meeting;
- who will be attending the meeting;
- that their contribution is valued. (A list of questions may help them to prepare for their contribution.)

**Running review meetings**

If the SENCO is to chair the meeting, as well as presenting a report, he or she will be responsible for running the meeting. This includes ensuring that all those attending feel that their contribution is valued, that everyone has an opportunity to present their view and that the time is effectively managed.
- Ensure that everyone is introduced and their professional role explained.
- Remind those attending of the format of the meeting, the agenda and the time allocated.
- If notes are to be taken, decide who should do this and ensure that this is discussed with parents.
- Keep to the time scale of the meeting.
- Allow time for discussion of parental concerns.
- Try to ensure agreement of all concerned regarding future action.
- At the end of the meeting summarise the main points and outcomes.

Examples of a letter of invitation to parents, a list of parent and pupil questions and an IEP review form are included in the Appendixes.

# Partnership with parents

Most schools have well-established and successful systems for involving parents in the education of their children. In liaising with the parents of children with SEN, schools may wish to review their present arrangements for parental partnership and decide where they might be extended. Whatever arrangements are made they should be set in a way which will encourage trust and confidence. Parents need to feel that the knowledge of their child that they bring, and the contributions that they make to review meetings and in supporting their child's education at home, are valued by all the professionals with whom they come into contact.

Establishing effective channels of communication with some parents who have had negative experiences of relationships with schools may prove difficult and may have to be worked at over long periods of time.

## Establishing contact with parents

Schools have many channels for contact with parents and for opening the lines of communication. These include:
- school brochure;
- parent booklets;
- school reports;
- home visits;
- telephone calls;
- letters;
- home–school diaries;
- newsletters;
- parent noticeboards;
- open evenings;
- meetings, both formal and informal;
- coffee mornings;
- special events;
- parent involvement in activities such as period reading.

## Providing information, partnership and access

The *Code of Practice,* in paragraphs 2:28 to 2:33, outlines recommendations for partnership with parents of children with SEN, paragraph 2:33 listing the arrangements which should be in place. These are divided into the three areas of information, partnership, and access for parents.
- Information:    on school policy;
  on support within school and available within the LEA;
  on parental contribution to assessment and decision making;
  on services provided by the LEA;
  on voluntary groups which might provide information, advice or counselling.

- Partnership:   arrangements for recording and acting on parental concerns;
  procedures for involving parents when a concern is expressed;
  arrangements to include parents' views in assessment and reviews.
- Access:   to information in the community language;
  to information on tape for parents with literacy or communication difficulties;
  to a parents' room or other arrangements in school to make parents feel confident and comfortable.

The areas of information and access are obviously linked. The information which parents will need will include that relevant to the individual school and also that relating to LEA policies and procedures. The LEA's information may be available from a central source as a pack giving details of the services by the LEA and procedures for statutory assessment. Some LEAs have appointed Parent Partnership Officers who have undertaken the preparation of such information.

In developing the policy for SEN, schools will have considered the issues related to effective partnership with parents. Questions which the school might need to address could include:
- How can we ensure that information relating to special needs reaches the parents who need it?
- Do parents feel that they can approach the school at any time if they have a concern?
- Do parents know who to contact about special needs?
- What channels do we use for communicating between home and school?
- How do we communicate with parents if we have a concern about their child?
- Do we have effective methods of gathering information from parents?
- Are parents actively involved in IEPs?
- Are review meetings organised in a way which supports parental contribution?

A variety of responses is possible to these questions depending on the school's present arrangements and the phase of education. In establishing a system for contact if either the parents or the school has a concern about a pupil's progress, the school will need to decide if the first contact should be through the child's class teacher/form tutor, the SENCO, the head of year in a secondary school or the headteacher. It is important that there is consistency of approach for both the parents and the school staff. The system chosen will depend on the phase and the size of the school, but all staff need to be aware of the procedures to be followed.

### Expressing an initial concern to parents

Contacting a parent to express concern regarding their child will obviously need to be handled sensitively. In some primary schools parents are encouraged to come into the school with their pupils at the start of the day and parents may be able to be approached then. For others it may be a telephone call, or part of a parents' meeting. If communication is in writing, it could be by a message in the home–school diary or a short note asking a parent to contact the school, but without causing alarm.

### Overcoming barriers

When there is a meeting with parents it is important to find somewhere for the meeting that ensures there are no interruptions and that the conversation cannot be overheard by people passing by. Some fortunate primary schools have parents' rooms, but in others it may be necessary to use the headteacher's office or the library. In secondary schools there are usually more offices and small meeting rooms which might be used for this purpose.

Whatever system for meeting or talking is established, the parent should be made to feel at ease, confident both in the confidentiality of the meeting and in the value put on the contribution they are making to it. Most teachers enjoy excellent relationships with most parents and can readily put them at their ease, but if parents have serious concerns about their child they may find it difficult to express them and teachers need to recognise that there may be barriers to communication.

Although most teachers are not trained counsellors, they can bring many skills to their work with parents:
* good listening skills;
* confidentiality;
* a non-judgemental response;
* honesty combined with tact;
* understanding;
* mutual respect;
* sharing of information.

Schools may decide that they wish to develop a leaflet giving information relating to the school's response to special needs, or to produce information on tape or even a video. In some schools parents of pupils with identified SEN have an opportunity to meet with the SENCO prior to the child's entry into the school. This meeting can help to establish relationships and provide an invaluable opportunity for an exchange of information, at transfer between primary and secondary school as well as prior to primary school entry. As already mentioned, Appendix 2 provides a list of questions which could be used as the basis of gathering information from parents regarding their child's needs, and information relating to parental involvement in IEPs and contributions to review meetings can be found in the relevant sections.

As part of its response to the *Code of Practice,* NASEN has produced a policy paper, 'Supporting Parents', which was ratified by its General Assembly. NASEN has also set up a Parental Partnership Interest Group, details of which are available from NASEN headquarters, the address of which is included in the reference pages.

# Links with other schools and transition between schools

A smooth transition into school and between schools is desirable for all pupils including those with SEN. The efficient transfer of information is essential to the SENCO in achieving this. This involves the gathering of information before a pupil enters the school and the transfer of information when the pupil changes schools or enters another phase of education, as well as establishing personal contacts with those who know the pupil best. For the SENCO this might involve:
- home visits;
- pre-school visits by pupil and/or parents;
- contact with agencies such as health and social services;
- liaison with pre-school playgroups and nurseries;
- attendance at case conferences and/or review meetings;
- visits to feeder schools to talk to staff and SENCO;
- co-ordination of information for teaching and support staff.

### Transfer of information between schools
Transfer of information between schools will probably include:
- SEN records, including statement, review records etc.;

- pupil profiles/records of achievement;
- details of IEPs;
- present levels of support and funding for statemented pupils.

Some local authorities and clusters of schools have developed transfer documents for pupils with SEN as an addition to the normal school records. This is worth considering, as a common format, agreed by those sending and receiving, should ensure that all appropriate information is transferred. This should only need to be quite brief as its main purpose is to alert the receiving school to the pupil's main difficulties and to give an overview of the information which is appended. An example of a proforma for this purpose is included in Appendix 13.

### Linking mainstream and special schools
Links with other schools can include both mainstream and special schools. Some special schools have strong links with mainstream schools in their area and integration of pupils is established, varying from a single session to a shared placement between schools. The success of such integration depends both on the ethos of the schools involved and the funding available to support the integration process.

Even in situations where there is no integration of pupils it is useful for SENCOs in mainstream schools to make regular contact with their special school colleagues, perhaps via SENCO or school cluster meetings, to share and exchange information regarding good practice, resources and research.

Links with other mainstream schools may include feeder primary schools, particularly in relation to pupils prior to transfer, and also other schools in a cluster or consortium, possibly via SENCO meetings. Any forum which enables SENCOs to share expertise and experience should be explored and valued, as it is often through these informal contacts that useful ideas and strategies can be developed.

# Working with outside agencies

How can the SENCO make the best use of the time spent working with outside agencies? There will be some agencies with which the SENCO has little contact and others, such as LEA support services or psychological services, with which he or she has regular meetings. Whether contacts are frequent or infrequent, systems will need to be set up which work effectively for each individual school.

**Making a list of organisations**
Firstly, make a list of the organisations the school already works with, including the name of the contact and the address and telephone number where they can be reached. It is also useful to record the times when they are usually available in the office as this can save wasted telephone calls. Such a list might include:

*LEA contacts*
- Psychological Service;
- Learning Support Service;
- Behaviour Support Service;
- Pupil Referral Units;
- Specialist Support Services for Visually and Hearing Impaired Pupils;
- Education Welfare/Education Social Workers;
- Parent Partnership Officers;
- LEA Education Officers for Special Educational Needs;
- LEA Inspector Adviser for SEN.

*Health service contacts*
- School Medical Officer;
- Speech and Language Therapists;
- Physiotherapists.

*Social Services*
Other agencies might include some of the following:
- Careers and Youth Services;
- voluntary agencies;
- special needs groups;
- pre-school groups.

The list should be kept updated and accessible, and from the knowledge of each particular school and locality, added to as appropriate. For those agencies with which there is only limited or intermittent contact, the SENCO should try to establish exactly what services they can offer and how best to access them. The SENCO should share information with other SENCOs and gather information from parents, particularly regarding voluntary groups with which they may be involved. In this way the range of expertise on which to call will be extended. A useful list of addresses of voluntary groups and organisations can be found in the booklet 'Special Educational Needs: a Guide for Parents' (DfE, 1994).

## Getting the most from agencies

The agencies with which the school is most likely to have more regular contacts are those such as LEA support services and psychological services. The way in which these contacts are organised will partly depend on the systems in place within the LEA regarding the delegation of funding. In those LEAs where funding is still centrally held, the service is likely to be free at the point of delivery. In others, where funding has been wholly or partially delegated to schools, the services may be purchased directly or via a 'quota' system allocating specific amounts of time to the school, additional time being purchased directly.

Whichever of these systems operates within the particular LEA, it is important to make the most of the school's entitlement, both in terms of time allocated and the services received.

Some of the services will relate to statutory work, such as contributions to assessment and Annual Reviews, others to non-statutory advice and support, and others to direct work with pupils.

## Support services checklist

The following checklist can be used to review the way in which work is done at present, and as a way of establishing priorities:

- What is your entitlement to each specialist service provided by the LEA?
- If you buy direct, how much funding is available?
- Have you written details of the services offered? (If not, ask for them.)
- Have you provided the service with details of your school systems and personnel?
- What is the cost and time allocation for each type of visit?
- If you are entitled to regular visits, how frequent will they be and how long will each visit last?
- What information does each service require from the school, prior to a visit?
- What follow-up services are provided between visits?
- Is telephone support available?

## Making the most of support service visits

Having established entitlement to visits or how much time can be bought, the SENCO should consider how to make the most of each visit.

- Clearly establish the purpose of the visit.
- Make sure you have all the necessary paperwork ready.
- If a pupil is to be assessed, make sure that the pupil is available at the appropriate time.
- List questions you wish to ask and items for discussion.
- Set clear agendas for liaison meetings.
- Manage time effectively in meetings and reviews.
- Keep notes of any actions agreed by you or the outside agency.
- If a regular meeting is cancelled, try to establish an alternative. Do not miss out.

## Giving feedback on services

In all this, the SENCO should try to establish good working relationships with the agencies which serve the school. Expectations should be made clear and the agency should be provided with the necessary support for them to fulfil their role efficiently. If the services received are unsatisfactory, this information should be fed back both to the headteacher and to the service line-manager. If purchasing the service, are there alternatives to explore? Similarly, if the service is working well, that should be related. The SENCO may also want to explore contributions to school INSET from the support services to raise awareness of all staff.

## Auditing the services received

An audit of the services the school receives will be useful in informing the governing body and LEA about the school's response to SEN. The following issues could be considered:

- Which service is most valued and why?
- Which services are least valued?
- How could relations with these services be improved?
- Is the time allocation from each service adequate?
- Are the reports and advice offered helpful and practical?
- Is follow-up support provided?
- Does each service represent good value for money?

If the SENCO considers that there is insufficient access to support services, he or she may wish to gather information to present to the governing body in order that they can consider the need for increased funding if this is available. If dissatisfied with the services the school receives, the SENCO must document all concerns and discuss them with the agency involved and with the headteacher or senior management.

### LEA education officer for SEN

The detail of responsibilities within this role will vary between LEAs, but this officer or officers will have responsibility for organising LEA provision for pupils with SEN. This will include the statutory assessment process and funding for special needs.

The SENCO will need to know:
- procedures and criteria for statutory assessment in the LEA;
- how resourcing is allocated to support pupils with statements;
- how non-statutory funding is allocated for special needs;
- arrangements for Annual Review meetings for statemented pupils.

Written information should be available from the LEA relating to all these, but the SENCO should also try to establish a personal contact with the officer responsible, especially if any of the procedures needs clarification.

### The LEA inspector/adviser for SEN

Who is the adviser, and has the SENCO met him/her? It would be useful to clarify what support is available from the adviser as part of any entitlement or service-level agreement and what services can be purchased. The SENCO can make contact with the adviser and discuss the school's particular needs, perhaps in relation to INSET. The inspector may be able to organise regular support meetings for SENCOs, or to provide financial support for professional development as part of an LEA initiative.

# Ofsted inspections

The *Education Reform Act 1989* introduced a cycle of inspections for all schools every four years. By now many schools will have experience of inspection under the Ofsted framework. In 1995 the framework for inspection was revised and three new handbooks published. The first is 'Guidance on the Inspection of Nursery and Primary Schools' (HMSO, 1995), with similar titles relating to secondary and special schools. The aim of the new handbook is to 'promote better reports through inspections which are more manageable by inspectors and less of a burden for schools.'

**Leadership and Management**
References to SEN are made throughout the schedule and guidance. Additional notes in section 6.1 (Leadership and Management) focus on 'the fulfilment of statutory responsibilities, and on the quality and effectiveness of the general oversight and day-to-day management arrangements shared by the governing body, headteacher and other staff' (HMSO, 1995). This section is identical in both the primary and secondary handbooks.

**Information for inspection**
The following list, based on section 6.1, outlines the information that the inspection team will be gathering together. It has been set out in the form of a series of questions which could act as a checklist for schools to use prior to inspection. The overarching question will relate to the school 'having regard' to the *Code of Practice* and to the relevant sections of the *Education Acts 1981, 1988* and *1993*. The inspectors will examine the school's policies and plans and have discussions with headteacher and governors, the SENCO, other staff, visiting specialists and (if possible) parents in order to gather the information they require.

- Has the governing body, in co-operation with the headteacher, determined the school's special needs policy and approach to SEN?
- Have they set up appropriate staffing and funding arrangements and do they maintain a general oversight of special needs provision?
- Has the governing body designated either the headteacher or an appropriate governor to be the 'responsible person' to oversee special needs in the school?
- Does the governing body's annual report inform parents of the success of the SEN policy, significant changes in it, allocation of resources over the previous year, and any consultations with the LEA, funding authority or other schools?
- Does the provision for special need permeate the school's organisational and curricular structures and practice in the school?
- Do all staff work closely with the SENCO?
- Do parents know who is their main point of contact and who is the school's 'responsible person'?
- Are resources, including staffing, managed effectively and efficiently to support the SEN policy and the pupils' identified needs?
- Are all staff aware of the procedures for identifying, assessing and providing for pupils with SEN?

- Is pupils' progress monitored, especially in relation to Annual Reviews and IEPs?
- Do assessment, recording and reporting satisfy statutory requirements?
- Is the use of specialist support from outside agencies well managed within the school?

As well as inspectors taking part in discussions with all those concerned with SEN and looking at policies and documentation, the school's response to special needs will be considered in each section of the inspection schedule.

In 'Part A, Aspects of the School', section 4, 'Educational standards achieved by pupils at the school', will look at the progress of pupils with SEN and evidence will include an analysis of statements, IEPs and Annual Reviews of a sample of pupils on the school's SEN register. Section 5, 'Quality of education provided', considering the teachers' use of assessment, will relate the assessment of the work of pupils with SEN to the targets set in IFPs, and also consider whether the curriculum meets the needs identified in the individual education plans and, for pupils at Stage 5, in statements and Annual Reviews.

# Professional development

All schools should have in place a policy relating to staff professional development. As a starting point to planning for the development of INSET for special needs it would be useful for the SENCO to undertake an informal audit of the school's present position in relation to training. This will enable the SENCO to present to the headteacher or governing body identified priorities which can be built into the staff development policy over a period of time.

### Considering training needs
Professional development needs may include those of the SENCO, school staff and governing body. In considering these in reverse order:

### *The governing body*
- Has the governing body received training in relation to its responsibilities within the *Code of Practice?*
- If not, is this already planned?

61

- Can this training be provided by the SENCO, or will it be via the LEA or another source?
- Are there cost implications for this?

## *Staff*

The training needs of staff should consider both teaching staff and classroom assistants. Some training may be appropriate to all staff, relating to whole school issues, other training might be more relevant to a subject area, a pastoral team, or new or newly qualified teachers, for example. It would be useful to survey all staff in order to identify their perceived priorities, which may not be identical to those of the SENCO. This could be by means of a questionnaire, a list for staff to rank in priority order, or form the focus of a discussion at a staff meeting.

Areas to be considered for in-service sessions could include:
- the *Code of Practice,* with particular reference to Stages 1 to 3;
- record keeping and report writing;
- developing IEPs;
- working with parents;
- differentiation;
- classroom-based assessment and monitoring;
- strategies to support pupils with literacy difficulties across the curriculum;
- specific learning difficulties;
- support for pupils with emotional and behavioural problems;
- physical and medical difficulties, e.g. asthma, diabetes, epilepsy;
- working with support staff and classroom assistants;
- information technology to support pupils with SEN.

Having identified priorities, the SENCO will need to liaise with the headteacher and/or the staff development officer to establish how these might be achieved. Thought will need to be given as to whether the training is appropriate for whole staff and will take place within the school or for selected staff who will attend at another venue. For both situations it will be necessary to consider who will provide the training, the cost implications and the timing of sessions.

## *Providers*

For whole staff this could be the SENCO or other staff, LEA providers such as inspection and advisory teams or support services, or outside providers such as those from colleges of further education or consultancies. For staff attending courses as individuals or groups it may be possible to access regional or national courses, such as those organised by special needs associations, as well as LEA in-service sessions.

*Cost implications*
The school will need to consider requests for special needs INSET in the context of the whole staff development budget. Funds are always limited and so whole school priorities must be clearly established together with the development of systems that help to ensure value for money, such as strategies to disseminate information from courses attended by individuals to all relevant staff.

*Timing*
Timing and funding are closely linked. If in-service sessions take place during the normal school day there are obviously cost implications in covering the timetables of the staff attending. For whole school in-service the possibilities include training days, twilight sessions, and input to established meetings such as staff and departmental meetings.

Whatever in-service programme is devised, there should be regular opportunity for review and reflection by SENCO and staff in order that efficient use is made of resources and that the INSET is not seen in isolation but effectively moves forward practice throughout the school.

**Professional development and support for the SENCO**
As well as organising an audit of the in-service needs of the whole school, the SENCO will need to consider his or her own needs in relation to professional development. An additional professional qualification, such as a diploma or degree, may be identified as a priority. If this is the case then the school will need to explore issues of funding and timing.

Some LEAs provide accredited training via twilight sessions, and funding for these and other courses such as distance learning packages may be available from GEST budgets. The SENCO will need to consider carefully the time commitment required for such training, in addition to an already heavy workload. An alternative could be a selection of modular courses relating to particular areas of interest which could lead towards a higher qualification at a later date.

### Delivering INSET

The SENCO may also develop his or her role as a provider of INSET to other staff. SENCOs frequently have a high degree of professional expertise but are reluctant, perhaps because of lack of confidence, to deliver in-service. Many LEAs and other providers now run sessions on in-service delivery and attendance at one of these could be very useful in developing the SENCO role.

### Joining an association

Membership of professional associations for SEN, such as NASEN, can also provide access to training and support, via local meetings and regional and national training courses. The professional journals of these associations enable SENCOs to keep in touch with recent research and developments in the field of SEN.

SENCO may also wish to consider setting up support groups in a local area or within a cluster or consortium of schools. Here SENCOs can share concerns and ideas, exchange experience and advice on strategies and resources, and develop initiatives in response to particular local needs. In some areas such groups are organised with the involvement of staff from the support services and this can help to enhance liaison and a sharing of expertise.

# Managing the SENCO Role

In addressing the issues raised in the previous chapters, the SENCO will need to consider how to develop as an effective manager. This will involve managing the responsibilities, managing time and managing stress. These three are in many ways almost inextricably interlinked.

### Managing the responsibilities

Managing the responsibilities may be seen as part of a whole school issue. Hopefully, some of the activities involved in the SENCO role will have raised the awareness of the whole staff and senior management to the range and level of responsibility which the SENCO holds.

In order to be able to respond effectively to the demands set by the *Code of Practice* the SENCO may need to develop their role in management decisions within the school. This might involve membership of a curriculum and/or pastoral committee in a secondary school, or as part of a management group in a primary.

The SENCO may also find it useful to attend INSET relating to management issues, if this is available. The SENCO also has a responsibility in managing the work of other staff, both teaching and non-teaching, who work with pupils with special needs. As well as organising timetables, advising on methodology and being involved in monitoring effectiveness, the SENCO is likely to be called on to support and advise staff.

## Time management
In order to be able to respond to the demands of the management role, the SENCO will need to consider his or her own time management. There are many publications which relate to time management and one useful reference is Hinson (1991), (see References, further reading and resources on page 67).

The important thing to remember is to use the time available effectively. It is useful to prioritise tasks, considering those imperative for the day, those which must be completed in the week, those which have a longer time span, and those which could be delegated.

When dealing with incoming paperwork, useful advice is, 'handle it once'. Decide if it requires immediate action, later reading, or filing. Two other ideas which aid effective time management are firstly, to try to block time for making and responding to phone calls and secondly, when arranging any meeting to allocate a time and to stick to it.

## Coping with stress
Effective time management and good organisational skills may help in dealing with the stress which the SENCO, in common with other staff in the school, may experience. Dealing with stress requires looking at both personal and organisational strategies.

At a personal level, talking to and sharing concerns with colleagues, asking for support from others and offering it, and developing good listening skills will help both the SENCO and other staff working with him or her.

At an organisational level it may be important for the SENCO to clarify and review the responsibilities of the post, to review training needs or to make use of the appraisal process in exploring how to use the time available more effectively.

It may also be useful to consider attending one of the stress management courses which are now provided by LEAs and other agencies, both with the aim of reducing personal stress and also in gaining a better understanding of the effects that stress might have on colleagues and how best to support them.

The post of SENCO can be very demanding and, at times, a very lonely one. It requires a constant response to the needs of pupils, staff, parents and other professionals. In order to be able to fulfil the role and develop, the SENCO needs the support of the headteacher, governing body and other staff, and a network of professional colleagues with whom to share the ups and downs of the job.

# References, further reading and resources

### General references
Bill, G (1995) *Governor's Guide to Special Educational Needs in Mainstream Schools,* NASEN: Tamworth.

Butt, N and Scott, E (1994) 'Individual Education Plans in Secondary Schools', *Support for Learning,* Volume 9, 1, NASEN: Tamworth.

DfE (1994) *Code of Practice on the Identification and Assessment of Special Educational Needs,* Department for Education: London.

DfE (1994) *Special Educational Needs: A Guide for Parents,* Department for Education: London.

DfE (1994) *Special Educational Needs Tribunal: How to Appeal,* Department for Education: London.

Ofsted (1995) *The Ofsted Handbook: Guidance on the Inspection of Secondary Schools,* HMSO: London.

Ofsted (1995) *The Ofsted Handbook: Guidance on the Inspection of Nursery and Primary Schools,* HMSO: London.

### NASEN
The National Association for Special Educational Needs (NASEN) has a wide range of publications relating to SEN, many written by practitioners. The association also publishes two journals and a magazine which provide valuable information relating to current research and developments. Membership of NASEN provides these periodicals at a reduced cost, as well as providing an opportunity to join a local branch, and access to study courses and national interest groups.

Membership details and a list of publications are available from:
NASEN
NASEN House
4/5 Amber Business Village
Amber Close
Amington
Tamworth   B77 4RP.

## Policy Development
Gordon, M and Smith, H (1994) *Policy Development for Special Educational Needs: A Secondary School Approach,* NASEN: Tamworth.

Luton, K (1995) *Policy Development for Special Educational Needs: A Primary School Approach,* NASEN: Tamworth.

## INSET
Caswell, J and Pinner, S (1995) *Special Educational Needs: Assistants and Teachers,* Northumberland County Council.
This is a ten-unit package aimed at providing training for classroom assistants working with a teacher partner.

Visser, J (1993) *Differentiation: Making it Work,* NASEN: Tamworth.
Useful for whole school INSET and as a start for subject departments.

## Individual education plans
Warin, S (1995) *Implementing the Code of Practice: Individual Education Plans,* NASEN: Tamworth.

## Time management
Hinson, M (1991) 'A survival guide to time management and the management of meetings', *Teachers and Special Educational Needs: Coping with Change,* Longman.

## Assessment and programme planning
'Early Years Easy Screen', NFER, Windsor.
Baseline assessment for children starting school. Identifies strengths and needs and gives suggestions for follow-up activities.

'Middle Infant Screening Test and Forward Together', NFER, Windsor.
Provides diagnostic information on listening and literacy skills, together with a teaching programme which actively involves parents.

'Early Mathematics Diagnostic Kit', NFER, Windsor.
An individually administered test for pupils aged 4 to 8 years that can be used with older pupils with learning difficulties. It provides a diagnostic assessment of early difficulties in mathematics, covering all the major areas including language.

'QUEST', NFER, Windsor.
A screening test in reading and mathematics for pupils between 6 and 8+ years, with additional diagnostic materials for those pupils identified as having difficulties.

'Skillteach', PAVIC Publications, Sheffield Hallam University.
A resource pack which provides a diagnostic assessment of reading difficulties and a programme which integrates phonic skills, high frequency words, context skills and spelling. The programme is supported by photocopiable sheets and a comprehensive manual with detailed notes on multisensory strategies.

'Individual Reading Analysis' (age range 5.6 to 10 years) and 'New Reading Analysis' (age range 7 to 9+ years), NFER-Nelson, Windsor.
Individual oral reading tests providing a diagnostic analysis of reading strategies using miscue analysis.

'Spelling in Context', NFER, Windsor.
A useful resource in assessing spelling development and in planning a programme.

'The Aston Index', LDA, Wisbech.
A battery of tests covering visual and auditory discrimination, received and expressive language, motor co-ordination, laterality, and written language, reading and spelling. Useful in assessing the strengths and weaknesses of pupils with specific learning difficulties.

# Appendixes

**The following pages may be photocopied for use within the school which purchases this book.**

# PROCEDURES, PRACTICE AND GUIDANCE FOR SENCOs

## Appendix 1
## Letter to parents expressing concern

Dear .............,

I am sorry that I have been unable to contact you personally.

I have recently spoken with ............'s class teacher who is concerned that ............ is having some difficulty with ............... . His/her teacher may give ............ some extra help and support as it is needed and we will monitor his/her progress carefully and will keep you informed.

If you would like to talk to us about this we would be very pleased to hear from you. Perhaps you feel that you would like to do something to help at home.

Please would you sign the slip below and return it to me so that we know that you have received this letter. Please add any information or comments that you think would be helpful.

Yours sincerely,


SENCO.

------------------------------------------------------------------------

Name of child ............................    Class/Tutor group ..............
I have received your letter concerning support for my child and monitoring of his/her progress.

*Comments and additional information*


.......................... Parent/Carer    Date .................

# PROCEDURES, PRACTICE AND GUIDANCE FOR SENCOs

**Appendix 2**
**Questions which might form the basis of an interview with parents, or guidelines for a written contribution, following an expression of concern in school**

In answering the following questions you will be giving us useful information which will help us in deciding how best to support your child in school.

## 1. The early years
Is there anything about your child's early years that you think it is important for us to know?
What was he/she like as a young baby?
Did he/she walk, talk and generally make progress as you would expect?
Were there any sleep problems?
Did he/she have any particular health problems?
Did you have any worries about him/her then?

## 2. School
Were there any difficulties when your child started school or changed schools?
Does your child talk to you about school?
Do you think he/she enjoys school?
Are some days more enjoyable than others?
Is there any reason for this that you are aware of?
How do you feel your child is getting on at school?
Which things does he/she find particularly easy or difficult?

## 3. Your child now
Does your child have any health problems now?
Does he/she have any problems with sight or hearing?
Does he/she eat and sleep well?
Is he/she happy at home?
What does he/she like to do at home?
Does he/she ride a bike, enjoy sports?
Does he/she get on well with brothers and sisters and others in the family?
Does he/she have many friends?
Do you have any worries about your child?
How do you think we can best help?
Would you like to help your child at home?
Is there any help you or your family would like?
Is there anything else you think it would be useful for us to know?

© Hazel Smith, 1996
NASEN Enterprises Ltd.

# PROCEDURES, PRACTICE AND GUIDANCE FOR SENCOs

## Appendix 3
### Invitation to parents to attend a review meeting

Name of pupil ............................... Date of birth .................
Date of last review meeting .................

Dear ............,

As you know we regularly review ....................'s progress and I would like to invite you to the next review meeting.

It will be held on ........................ at ...............am/pm. The meeting should last no longer than ........................ .

Other people who have been invited are:
                    (name)                    (role)


We value the contribution that you will be able to bring to the meeting. I have attached a list of questions that you might like to think about and on which we would appreciate your views.

Please would you return the attached slip to let me know that you are able to attend.

Yours sincerely,

SENCO.

------------------------------------------------------------------------

Name of pupil .................... Review meeting to be held on ...............
I am able to come to the review meeting.
Parent/Carer........................

© Hazel Smith, 1996
NASEN Enterprises Ltd.

# PROCEDURES, PRACTICE AND GUIDANCE FOR SENCOs

**Appendix 4**
**Questions for parents to consider before a review meeting**

1. How do you feel about your child's general progress over the past year?

2. Do you think he/she has made progress in each of the targets set at the last review?

3. Have you been able to help at home? If so, how have you got on?

4. Is there any new information about your child that you think it would be helpful for us to know?

5. Do you have any particular worries about your child that you would like to discuss?

6. Do you think the present arrangements to support your child are going well?

7. Is there anything that you think should be changed?

8. What do you think your child should be aiming to achieve next?

9. Would you like to help with the new targets at home?

10. Have you talked to your child about his/her progress? What did he/she say?

© Hazel Smith, 1996
NASEN Enterprises Ltd.

# PROCEDURES, PRACTICE AND GUIDANCE FOR SENCOs

## Appendix 5
## Questions to be discussed with the pupil prior to a review meeting

1. How do you feel you are getting on in school at the moment?

2. What do you enjoy most?

3. Which activities/subjects do you think you are best at?

4. Which activities/subjects do you find difficult?

5. Can you explain what makes them hard?

6. What things do you find easy?

7. Do you think you have met the targets planned at your last review?

8. How do you feel about the help you are getting at the moment?

9. Is there anything about the way you are helped that you would change if you could?

10. What would you like to achieve before your next review?

11. Is there anything else you think it would be useful for us to know?

12. Would you like to come to the review meeting to talk about these questions?

© Hazel Smith, 1996
NASEN Enterprises Ltd.

# PROCEDURES, PRACTICE AND GUIDANCE FOR SENCOs

## Appendix 6
### Special Educational Needs Register

School:                          Date:

| Name | Date of birth | Yr Gp | Area of need | | | | | | Date included on register | | | | |
|---|---|---|---|---|---|---|---|---|---|---|---|---|---|
| | | | L | B | P/M | H | V | S/L | Stage 1 | Stage 2 | Stage 3 | Stage 4 | Stage 5 |
| | | | | | | | | | | | | | |
| | | | | | | | | | | | | | |
| | | | | | | | | | | | | | |
| | | | | | | | | | | | | | |
| | | | | | | | | | | | | | |
| | | | | | | | | | | | | | |
| | | | | | | | | | | | | | |
| | | | | | | | | | | | | | |
| | | | | | | | | | | | | | |
| | | | | | | | | | | | | | |
| | | | | | | | | | | | | | |
| | | | | | | | | | | | | | |
| | | | | | | | | | | | | | |
| | | | | | | | | | | | | | |
| | | | | | | | | | | | | | |
| | | | | | | | | | | | | | |
| | | | | | | | | | | | | | |
| | | | | | | | | | | | | | |
| | | | | | | | | | | | | | |
| | | | | | | | | | | | | | |
| | | | | | | | | | | | | | |
| | | | | | | | | | | | | | |

| | |
|---|---|
| L | Learning |
| B | Behaviour |
| P/M | Physical/Medical |
| H | Hearing |
| V | Vision |
| S/L | Speech/Language |

Further details can be found in the individual records for each pupil

_____ Headteacher

_____ SENCO

© Hazel Smith, 1996
NASEN Enterprises Ltd.

75

# PROCEDURES, PRACTICE AND GUIDANCE FOR SENCOs

**Appendix 7**

## Special Educational Needs Record

SCHOOL: _____

Name _____ Date of birth _____

Parent/carers _____

Address _____

---

Concerns: (if more than one, list main concern first)

Strengths:

Date:

Parents contacted (date)          Information from parents attached (date)

School records [    ]    Health Services [    ]    Education Welfare [    ]

Pupils [    ]    Social Services [    ]    Other _____

**STAGE 1**    Included on SEN Register at Stage 1 on _____

Classroom strategies in response to concern:

Parental involvement:

---

Review date 1: _____ Reviewed by:

Recommendations following review:

Review date 2: _____ Reviewed by:

Outcome of review          Additional information attached: [    ]

Removed from register [    ]

Continue at Stage 1 [    ]

Move to Stage 2 [    ]

Parents consulted on: _____

# PROCEDURES, PRACTICE AND GUIDANCE FOR SENCOs

**Appendix 8**

## Record of Concern

Date _____

Pupil's name _____          Class/Form _____

Main area of concern:




Photocopy of work attached     Yes/No

Present classroom intervention:




Pupil's strengths:




Teacher expressing concern          _____

Subject area (if appropriate)          _____

Concern already discussed with          _____

A copy of this form has been sent to:          Class teacher/Form teacher
(delete as applicable)                                    Head of year
                                                                     Deputy head
                                                                     Headteacher

© Hazel Smith, 1996
NASEN Enterprises Ltd.

## Appendix 9

### Individual Education Plan

**STAGE 2**

Pupil's name: _____ Number of IEPs at Stage 2: _____

Class/Tutor Group: _____ Start date for this IEP: _____

| Targets: |
| --- |
| |
| Activities/Resources/Timing/People involved: |
| |
| Monitoring/Assessment: |
| |

IEP agreed by:
    SENCO: _____      Review Date: _____
    Class/subject teacher: _____      Outcome of review:
    Support teacher: _____      Return to Stage 1:    Y/N*
    Classroom assistant: _____      Continue at Stage 2:   Y/N*
    External specialist: _____      Move to Stage 3:    Y/N*
    Parent: _____      Make referral to:_____
    Pupil: _____      _____

*Please delete as appropriate.

© Hazel Smith, 1996
NASEN Enterprises Ltd.

# PROCEDURES, PRACTICE AND GUIDANCE FOR SENCOs

## Individual Education Plan

### STAGE 2/3

Pupil's name: _____    Date of IEP: _____

Class/Tutor Group: _____    Number of IEPs at this stage: _____

| Targets: | Activities and resources: |
|---|---|
| | |

Teaching arrangements: including staff involved, amount of time, and frequency and location

| Parental involvement | External specialist involvement (if appropriate): |
|---|---|
| | |

Monitoring/Assessment arrangements:

IEP agreed by:
  Class/subject teacher: _____    Review Date: _____
  SENCO: _____    Outcome of review: _____
  Support teacher: _____    _____
  Support assistant: _____    _____
  External specialist: _____    _____
  Parent: _____    _____
  Pupil: _____    _____

## Individual Education Plan - Stage 2

Name: _____

Class/Tutor group: _____

Numbers of IEPs at this stage: _____

Date of this IEP: _____

| Targets | Activities and resources | People involved | Frequency | Monitoring/ Assessment |
|---|---|---|---|---|
| 1. | | | | |
| 2. | | | | |
| 3. | | | | |

IEP agreed by: (signatures as appropriate)

SENCO: _____
Class/subject teacher: _____
Support teacher: _____
Classroom assistant: _____
External specialist: _____
Parent: _____
Pupil: _____

Review Date: _____

Outcome of review:
Return to Stage 1: _____
Continue at Stage 2: _____
Move to Stage 3: _____
Make referral to: _____

# PROCEDURES, PRACTICE AND GUIDANCE FOR SENCOs

## Appendix 10
### Individual Education Plan (Secondary)

Name:_____          Stage 2/3

Form: _____          Date of this IEP: _____

Number of IEPs at this stage: _____

| Targets<br>1.<br>2.<br>3. | | |
|---|---|---|
| Activities/Resources<br><br>1.<br><br><br>2.<br><br><br>3. | Subject areas/staff involved | Monitoring/ Assessment |
| External agency involvement | | |
| Parental involvement | | |

Review date _____          Outcome of review:
                                   Continue at Stage          2/3
                                   Move to Stage              1/2
                                   Consider statutory assessment   Y/N

© Hazel Smith, 1996
NASEN Enterprises Ltd.

# PROCEDURES, PRACTICE AND GUIDANCE FOR SENCOs

**Appendix 11**

## Monitoring of Progress

Pupil's name　_____

Class/Tutor group　_____

Stage　　　　1　2　3　4　5

Information required by (date) _____

Member of staff contributing information_____

Subject _____

Please comment on:

Response to support strategies:

Progress towards IEP targets:

Any further concerns:

Please add any additional information as necessary:

© Hazel Smith, 1996
NASEN Enterprises Ltd.

# PROCEDURES, PRACTICE AND GUIDANCE FOR SENCOs

## Appendix 12
### Individual Education Plan - Review

Name: _____    Stage: _____

Class/Tutor group: _____    Date of commencement of this IEP: _____

Number of IEPs at this stage: _____

| | |
|---|---|
| Progress made (related to targets): | |
| Views of parent: | Views of pupil: |
| Comments from external specialist (if appropriate): | Additional information: |
| Outcome of review:<br><br>Pupil remains at Stage _____<br>Pupil moves to Stage _____ | Recommendations for next IEP: |

Those involved in review:

SENCO: _____    Others: _____

Class/Subject teacher _____    _____

Parent _____

Pupil _____

External specialist _____    Date _____

© Hazel Smith, 1996
NASEN Enterprises Ltd.

# PROCEDURES, PRACTICE AND GUIDANCE FOR SENCOs

**Appendix 13**

_____ School

**Transfer Information**

Pupil's name _____ Primary school _____

Date of birth _____ Primary school contact _____

Stage   1   2   3   4   5   (circle as appropriate)

If statemented:   Date of last Annual Review _____

   Present level of support/additional funding _____

External agency(ies) involved:   Contact:

Main areas of concern:

Support provided by school:

Pupil's strengths:

National Curriculum: Level
English
Mathematics
Science

Appended:   SEN records:   1   2   3   4   5
   Present Individual Education Plan: _____
   Copy of Statement: _____
   Annual Review: _____

Additional information from: _____

© Hazel Smith, 1996
NASEN Enterprises Ltd.

84